Description and Comparison in Cultural Anthropology

THE LEWIS HENRY MORGAN LECTURES/1968

presented at
The University of Rochester
Rochester, New York

Description and Comparison in Cultural Anthropology

WARD H. GOODENOUGH, *University of Pennsylvania*

ALDINE PUBLISHING COMPANY, *Chicago*

First published 1970 by
Aldine Publishing Company
529 South Wabash Avenue
Chicago, Illinois 60605

Library of Congress Catalog Card Number 70–115937
SBN 202–01079–1
Printed in the United States of America

ACKNOWLEDGMENTS

THE AUTHOR gratefully acknowledges permission by the publishers to repro-
duce the following quotations:
(on p. 2) from C. Kluckhohn, "Universal Categories of Culture," in
A. L. Kroeber, ed., *Anthropology Today: An Encyclopedic Inventory,*
p. 521, The University of Chicago Press, copyright 1953 by The University
of Chicago;
(on pp. 3, 4, 125) from G. P. Murdock, *Social Structure,* pp. 1–3, 8, 214,
copyright 1949 by The Macmillan Company;
(on p. 12) from M. Fortes, "Introduction," in M. Fortes, ed., *Marriage in
Tribal Societies,* p. 8, Cambridge Papers on Social Anthropology No. 3,
copyright by the Cambridge University Press;
(on p. 62) from R. F. Gray, "Sonjo Bride-Price and the Question of
African 'Wife-Purchase',", and (on p. 91) from D. M. Schneider, "Yap
Kinship Terminology and Kin Groups," reproduced by permission of the
American Anthropological Association from the *American Anthropologist,*
vol. 62, 1960, p. 43, and vol. 55, 1953, p. 231, respectively.

FOR RUTH

Contents

Foreword

THE LEWIS HENRY MORGAN LECTURES are intended to commemorate both the man and his work,[1] the latter being viewed as having provided an admirably broad and substantial base for anthropologists of later generations to build upon, as they have done and continue to do in diverse ways.

Professor Goodenough's work, in the past and in this book particularly, emphasizes the vitality and fruitfulness of Morgan's contributions. Not only do these Lectures carry forward Morgan's interests in kinship; they reflect as well his concern for comparative studies undertaken with the aim of ultimately understanding mankind.

Moreover, Professor Goodenough has elucidated recent developments in the collection, analysis, and presentation of cultural data in ways that make it easier for all of us to see how his methods (in themselves specialized) can broaden and deepen our understanding of culture and of man.

Morgan, himself a pioneer in method, would surely have been an attentive auditor—and discussant—at Professor Goodenough's

1. In Forewords to earlier volumes of this series, most recently in Professor Meyer Fortes' *Kinship and the Social Order* (1969), there are brief paragraphs about Lewis Henry Morgan's connection with the University of Rochester and about the initiation of the Morgan Lectures in 1963. Interested readers can refer to previous volumes for these notes, which need not be repeated here.

Lectures, and in his seminars and the less formal events in which he participated while at Rochester, and to which he contributed so much. Those faculty and students who were privileged to hear him on these occasions can testify not only to the interest stimulated by Professor Goodenough's presentations, but to his generous responsiveness in the give and take of discussion.

This volume is an expanded version of the Lewis Henry Morgan Lectures delivered at the University of Rochester, April 2 to 11, 1968.

Alfred Harris
Department of Anthropology
University of Rochester

Preface

THE OCCASION for this little book was a series of four Lewis Henry Morgan Lectures at the University of Rochester during two weeks in April 1968. In the year and a half since, I have expanded and revised the text prepared for the first three lectures and have newly written the fourth, originally delivered from notes. I have been able to take account of some of the literature that has appeared in the interim, and I have taken advantage of seminar discussions with students and faculty at the University of Rochester.

The third lecture draws heavily on work in componential analysis sponsored by a research grant from the National Institute of Mental Health (Grant No. MH-06126). The other lectures are largely distillations from courses I have taught in social organization, and they owe much to the searching questions of students.

My debt to Professor George P. Murdock is obviously great. I was his student when he was writing his landmark work *Social Structure*. It has served as a point of departure in the development of my own thinking about the matters I discuss here. And it was as his student that I first began to formulate in my doctoral dissertation the point of view I present in the fourth lecture.

Finally, I must thank Alfred and Grace Harris, along with their colleagues and students at the University of Rochester, for a most enjoyable and stimulating experience.

Introduction

HUMAN SOCIETIES, anthropologists maintain, despite their many forms and diverse customs, are all alike in being expressions of mankind's common human nature. Anthropology, of course, aims to clarify just what that nature is. The self-examination this search requires is not easy. Our theories are almost inevitably colored by the image we would like to have of ourselves, not only as men in contrast with animals, but as particular men in contrast with other men. The history of anthropology has been a continual struggle to get beyond the ethnocentric assumptions by which we pride ourselves as civilized, Christian, and so on, and to see human phenomena other than through the lenses to which our society's customs have habituated us.[1]

The study of social organization has just such a history. The topics discussed in this book have commanded more attention from anthropologists since the days of Bachofen, McLennan, Maine, Morgan, and Westermarck than most other topics one is likely to name. Yet anthropologists are still arguing over fundamental concepts and are still engaged in the search for definitions they can apply to all societies. Indeed, every one of the things I shall discuss —marriage, family, descent, and kinship—poses a conceptual problem.

1. See, for example, Gould's (1963) analysis of ethnocentric bias in functional theory and interpretation. (Complete references are given under author's name and date of publication under the heading "References" at the end of the book.)

1

It does so because all along we have been taking for granted that we know what these things are. They are all phenomena that we recognize in our own society without difficulty most of the time, and we can talk with one another meaningfully about them. But when we go to other societies, these familiar concepts begin to be troublesome. It is difficult to decide what is marriage among the Nayar of southwestern India and what is kinship among the Trobriand Islanders.

But we have to find some set of terms that will enable us to describe other cultures with minimal distortion from ethnocentric cultural bias. And we need some set of universally applicable concepts that will enable us to compare cultures and arrive at valid generalizations about them. Fifteen years ago, Kluckhohn (1953: 521) spoke of this need, saying:

> Valid cross-cultural comparison could best proceed from the invariant points of reference supplied by the biological, psychological and sociosituational "givens" of human life. These and their interrelations determine the likenesses in the broad categories and general assumptions that pervade all cultures because the "givens" provide foci around which and within which the patterns of every culture crystallize. Hence comparison can escape from the bias of any distinct culture by taking as its frame of reference natural limits, conditions, clues, and pressures.

In these lectures, I shall try to illustrate some of the difficulties we anthropologists have had in these related problems of description and comparison. I shall also try to describe the kind of approach I think promises to overcome these difficulties. The approach, I should hasten to add, is not a novel one. But it has not been fashionable among anthropologists and has only begun to be developed systematically.[2]

2. Buchler and Selby (1968) provide the most comprehensive discussion using the point of view I try to express here. Their book was not published until after these lectures were given. I have not been able, therefore, to take it as fully into account as I would like to have done. There is inevitably some overlap in what we have to say. But theirs is a textbook for advanced students and covers a wider range of topics. It has somewhat different immediate objectives and emphases. These lectures, therefore, tend to complement rather than duplicate what they have done.

1. Marriage and Family

In 1949 George P. Murdock wrote:

> THE *nuclear family* consists typically of a married man and woman with their offspring . . . [p. 1] The nuclear family is a universal human social grouping. Either as the sole prevailing form of the family or as the basic unit from which more complex familial forms are compounded, it exists as a distinct and strongly functional group in every human society . . . [p. 2] Whatever larger familial forms may exist, and to whatever extent the greater unit may assume some of the burdens of the lesser, the nuclear family is always recognizable and always has its distinctive and vital functions—sexual, economic, reproductive, and educational [p. 3].

Speaking of marriage and its relation to sexual privilege and economic cooperation between the sexes, Murdock observed:

> Sexual unions without economic cooperation are common, and there are relationships between men and women involving a division of labor without sexual gratification . . . but marriage

3

exists only when the economic and sexual are united into one relationship, and this combination occurs only in marriage. Marriage, thus defined, is found in every known human society. In all of them, moreover, it involves residential cohabitation, and in all of them it forms the basis of the nuclear family [p. 8].

Thus seen, marriage is a contractual union of a man and a woman and involves sexual privilege, economic cooperation, cohabitation, the production of children, and responsibility for the children's care, socialization, and education. If the marriage is fruitful, the resulting social unit is a nuclear or elementary family. Marriage is thus the social transaction that establishes a nuclear family. Other definitions of marriage—variously phrased as a union of a man and woman in which they are the jural father and mother of the children born to the woman (Malinowski 1930: 134–143; Radcliffe-Brown 1950:5) or in which the woman's children are regarded as their legitimate offspring (*Notes and Queries* 1951:110)—imply the same thing: marriage establishes the jural basis for a group consisting of a man, a woman, and their children, legitimizing the man's and woman's parenthood and assigning them whatever rights and responsibilities parenthood brings.

All this fits very well the prevalent view of what a family is and does in our own middle-class society. What we recognize, in fact, as the nuclear family in other societies is the social unit that comes closest to being the functional analogue of our own family. And we recognize as marriage whatever transaction functions to establish this social unit.

Since Murdock wrote, it has become clear that the nuclear or elementary family as he defined it is not universal. Writers have pointed to the Nayar castes of southwestern India (Gough 1959, 1961; Mencher 1965), to the kibbutz communities in Israel (Spiro 1954, Talmon 1965), and to the so-called matrifocal family in the Caribbean (Adams 1960) as societies or part societies in which traditional definitions, such as Murdock's, are inapplicable. The exceptions are few, and they appear to have arisen in response to special conditions. Murdock seems to be right in seeing the nuclear family as so convenient a social instrument for handling a bundle of universal human problems as to make its institutionalization almost inevitable. His comments (1949:11) on the functional efficacy of the nuclear family are not contradicted by the existence of a few societies in which the nuclear family is apparently absent, an absence that he, too, has acknowledged in his later work (1959).

The exceptions remain, however, and they make it clear that the elementary family is not the basic unit of human society that Murdock and others (e.g., Bell and Vogel 1960:2; Goode 1964) have taken it to be. We have been victims of our ethnocentrism, taking a functionally significant unit of our society—one that we regard as basic to our society—and treating the nearest functional equivalent elsewhere as if it were, in some fundamental way, the same thing.

For some purposes, there is nothing wrong with such a procedure. But if our purpose is to develop a set of concepts to describe and compare *all* human societies—*all* distinct cultural communities —then the traditional concepts of marriage and family are unsatisfactory, serving only as a negative standard of comparison, one that emphasizes degrees of difference from our own institutions and obscures what is common and basic to human societies generally.

The use of one's own culture as a negative standard lies behind the entire set of evolutionary sequences formulated by nineteenth-century theorists, Morgan (1877) prominently included. If we begin with ourselves as representing the most advanced state of human society and culture, then other societies can be readily conceived as falling on a continuum according to how similar in form to our family their nearest functionally equivalent institution appears to us. Nineteenth-century theorists assumed that if repeated application of this procedure to a number of functionally distinct institutions— family, marriage, religion, law, state, technology—resulted in a marked tendency for each society to occupy the same place relative to other societies on each scale, then this result would confirm their deductions about the evolution of civilization and would allow them to make valid inferences about the stages through which that evolution had progressed from the time when men first began to have a culture at all.[1] The expected correlations have not been realized.

1. Morgan (1877) postulated that forms of family, kinship, and political organization were thus associated with one another and with levels of technological sophistication and complexity. Tylor (1889) proposed the use of statistical indices to test empirically the validity of such postulated associations.

Assertions to the contrary by some anthropologists[2] are not supported by the increasing body of comparative data, which has now been brought together in a convenient reference book by Textor (1967). These data, however, are largely presented in terms of the old, ethnocentricly based concepts. Comparative study requires that we reëxamine the phenomena from other points of view.

This need has been recognized. Stephens (1963:4), for example, says that after a cross-cultural study he "was unable to arrive at a clear definition of the 'family'." Mogey (1963:5) comments on a symposium, "All these papers point to the necessity . . . to clarify the concept of the nuclear family." The inclusion of several independent functions in Murdock's definition of the family has been criticized as unworkable by Levy and Fallers (1959). Of marriage Nimkoff (1965:16) writes that its "earlier definition . . . which emphasized coresidence, coitus and economic cooperation is incomplete for cross-cultural purposes." Leach (1961:104) rightly emphasizes that "marriage is (to borrow Maine's phrase) 'a bundle of rights'," but he concludes unnecessarily "that all universal definitions of marriage are vain." Fox (1967) has dealt sensibly with some of the underlying considerations common to all human groups, but the conceptual and theoretical issues need further examination.

MARRIAGE

Her work with the Nayar led Kathleen Gough (1959) to reconsider the concept of marriage. In order to appraise her redefinition and illustrate the problem at hand, I shall briefly describe the traditional domestic institutions of the Nayar (Gough 1959, 1961; for recent changes see Nakane 1963).

The Nayar comprise a number of local castes or *jati* in southwestern India. They are landowners and in former times supplied the fighting men in the armies of the several kingdoms in the area. Estates in land were held collectively by groups of kinsmen related in the female line. The members of each such matrilineal corporation or *tāvari*, as it is called, lived together in a common household and operated a common domestic economy. The eldest male member was manager of the corporation's affairs. The men kept their

2. E.g., the assertion by Service (1962:107) that "the simplest, most rudimentary form of social structure, as a *structure* . . . is the patrilocal band."

belongings in the corporation house, took their meals there, and regarded it as their home. Several corporations related to one another
through a common ancestress and occupying the same neighborhood
formed an exogamous group called a *taravād*.

Before a girl reached menarche, she went through the ceremony
of *tāli*-tying, which elsewhere in India serves to join a man and girl
in a permanent union that fits well the traditional definition of marriage. But among the Nayar, the young man left the girl a few days
after the *tāli*-tying ceremony and was under no further obligation to
her. He might or might not have had sexual relations with her, in
accordance with her age, but he had sexual rights only for the
several days he remained with her. She and her future children were
obligated to mourn when he died, but they owed him nothing more.
The *tāli*-tying ceremony did not result in a relationship (after the
ceremony was over) in which there was continuing sexual privilege,
coresidence, and economic cooperation between the participants.
What it did was make the girl eligible to enter into sexual liaisons
with men approved by her *taravād* and establish her as an adult
female member of her *taravād*. It also satisfied the Hindu religious
requirement that a girl be "married"—have been through the Hindu
tāli-tying ceremony—before she reached menarche.

After the *tāli*-tying, another man might enter into a liaison with
the young woman, provided the men of her household approved of
him. He had to be from her *jati* or from one of higher ritual rank.
He could be a Nambudiri Brahman, if the girl's *jati* was a high-
ranking one. This *sambandham* liaison was a formal relationship,
marked by the man's obligatory gifts to the woman on three occasions each year. It entitled the man to spend nights with the
woman in her *tāvari* house. He had continuing sexual privileges,
but he had no economic obligations for her support. He did not
regard her apartment in her *tāvari* house as his home, nor did he
necessarily recognize her children as his own. A woman might have
such a liaison with more than one man at a time, the men arranging
their nocturnal visits so as not to conflict. The man with whom she
had been joined in the *tāli*-tying ceremony might become one of her
sambandham partners.

When a woman became pregnant, one or more men of appropriate caste had formally to acknowledge their possible paternity.
Otherwise, it was assumed she had been having relations with an in-

eligible man, and she and the child were expelled from their *taravād* and *jati*. A man acknowledged paternity by making gifts to the woman and to the midwife. He subsequently might take considerable interest in the child, but the child did not refer to him by the kinship term used for fathers in the patrilineal castes,[3] nor was the child obligated ritually to mourn his death. He had no obligations to socialize, educate, sponsor, or provide economically for the child. These usual parental obligations belonged to the men of the child's *tāvari*: the child's maternal uncles and older mother's sister's sons.

There were, then, three formal transactions. The first was the *tāli*-tying, which made a girl an adult and eligible to enter into sexual liaisons. The second established a liaison or *sambandham* relationship, which gave a man continuing sexual privileges and made the woman eligible to conceive and bear children. The third was the act of paternal recognition, which established that the child was the product of a legitimate sexual liaison and therefore entitled to be a member of its mother's *taravād* and *tāvari*.

In all human societies, it is necessary to have some means of determining when a woman is eligible for sexual relations and when she is eligible to bear children. The timing of these eligibilities does not always coincide. In all societies, there is need to know when a man is eligible to engage in sexual relations, too, and, if relevant, when he is eligible to beget children. And in all societies, there is need to determine who has sexual privileges with whom and on what occasions. Everywhere, finally, criteria of some kind are needed by which to determine where a child belongs, in what groups he has membership rights, and what adults are responsible for his maintenance, socialization, education, and for protecting his interests and enforcing his rights.

In the United States these universal requirements are ideally taken care of in two transactions. One of them, in our thinking the basic one, is the transaction we call *marriage*. The other is the registration of birth, in which responsibility for the child is allocated to a woman as *mother* and to a man as *father,* the two being ideally

---

3. This kinship term, *appan,* was reserved for the man who had engaged in the *tāli*-tying with the children's mother, if they happened to be personally acquainted with him (Gough 1961:358). Unless he had subsequently entered into a *sambandham* liaison with the mother, however, he had nothing to do with the acknowledgment of paternity and legitimation of the children.

already married to each other. Murdock, as we saw, asserted that most of these requirements are similarly handled in one basic transaction in all societies, the one that establishes a nuclear family and that we perceive as the fundamental analogue of our marriage. But the Nayar, we see, handle these matters in separate transactions: the *tāli*-tying, which makes a woman eligible for sexual relations; the *sandbandham,* which establishes concubicular rights; and the acknowledgment of paternity, which clears a child for membership in its *tāvari* and *taravād,* whose adult members are responsible for the child's maintenance, socialization, education, and legal rights in society. By Murdock's definition there is no nuclear family here and, therefore, no marriage. The basic social units in Nayar society are the matrilineal *tāvari* and, within them, the units consisting of a woman and her preadult children.

But the absence of a nuclear family organization need not mean that there are no transactions functioning in some respect like our own transaction of marriage. The difficulty in the traditional definitions has been the assumption that these transactions are universally linked with the establishment of a social group of a particular structural and functional kind. So let us ignore the kinds of social groups involved and look at the kinds of human social problems the transactions are intended to solve. The problems that concern us have to do with changes in people's eligibilities and entitlements as they relate to sexual reproduction and its resulting children.

In keeping with this approach, Kathleen Gough (1959) has offered a definition of marriage as a customary transaction that functions to establish the legitimacy of new-born children as acceptable members of society.[4] Because the *sambandham* relationship and acknowledgment of paternity with gifts function in this way among the Nayar, she saw them as the Nayar equivalent of our marriage. Certainly, in both Nayar and Anglo-American society,

---

4. Thus she broadens the definitions offered by Radcliffe-Brown (1950:5) and in *Notes and Queries* (1951:110). Both definitions stress legitimacy, linking marriage to the legitimation of children as the offspring of the husband and wife, rather than simply as members of society. Malinowski (1930:35) similarly associates legitimacy of conception with marriage and states (p. 140) that "marriage cannot be defined as the licensing of sexual intercourse, but rather as the licensing of parenthood." We shall see that marriage is, indeed, important for a cross-cultural definition of jural fatherhood, but not precisely in the way these writers have implied.

a child's acceptability as a proper member of society is in part dependent both on the mother's eligibility to bear children and on the acceptance of responsibility for the child's existence by a man who is eligible to be its genitor—one of the woman's *sambandham* partners among the Nayar and the woman's legal *husband* among ourselves. But two cases do not make a universal. The acceptability of a child is a matter requiring some means of determination in every society; but it need not involve a transaction between a man and a woman or any consideration of who is the genitor.

In Onotoa in the southern Gilbert Islands of Micronesia, for example, an unmarried woman is not eligible to bear children. A child born out of wedlock without acknowledged paternity has, at best, a marginal position in society. But if a man publicly acknowledges that he is the child's genitor, which he may or may not do as he chooses, the child acquires full rights in society and is an heir to the man's property equally with his other children.[5] Marriage is clearly not necessary for the legitimation of a child's rights to property and kindred in Onotoa.

A woman of Truk, also in Micronesia, becomes eligible to have sexual relations and to bear children simply by virtue of her having passed menarche.[6] Any children she bears thereafter are automatically members of her lineage and clan in good standing and, as such, legitimate members of society. They may be handicapped by having no paternal kinsmen, but they are not stigmatized in any way. The one criterion of acceptability is that the child not be seriously deformed physically. A deformed child is adjudged to be the offspring of a spirit rather than of a man. It is not a human being, and is therefore to be destroyed (Bollig 1927:86).

There is a transaction in Truk that all authorities have labeled marriage. In it a man acquires continuing sexual rights in a woman, and she in him; he acquires economic rights and duties vis-à-vis the

5. I have personal knowledge, for example, of a girl born out of wedlock to a woman who at the time was ineligible to have children. The genitor acknowledged paternity and was subsequently killed in World War II without having married. The girl inherited his sizable estate and in 1951 was regarded as a prize marital catch, having been betrothed to a man of high social rank in her community.

6. Except when otherwise noted, all references to Truk are based on my own ethnographic study in the community of Romónum in 1947 and 1964–65.

woman; and he acquires the duty of providing for the welfare, socialization, and education of all the children the woman has already borne and will yet bear for as long as he remains her husband. Trukese regard the children of one woman as an indivisible unit, no matter how many fathers they may have. Property acquired by one child from his particular father becomes the corporate property of all his mother's children, as well, under the authority of whoever among them is eldest. If a woman's first child is born before she gets a husband, the child will acquire equal rights in the property that her subsequent children get from their father. Moreover, he will become administrator of that property in the collective name of the sibling group, which he, as eldest, heads.

By Gough's definition, then, we find marriage but no conjugal families among the Nayar, and we find conjugal families but no marriage in Truk.

Nevertheless, Gough has moved in the right direction in that she looks for a universal problem, one that all societies must handle; but she has selected one whose solution does not require a transaction involving a man and a woman. To achieve a generally applicable definition of marriage, we must find a universal human interest that relates in some way to sexual reproduction and that does require such a transaction.

Sexual access is the only human concern I can find that meets this requirement. That it should do so is itself a reflection of several general human characteristics. One is the tendency to form continuing, affect-laden relationships. The reasons for this tendency are imperfectly understood, but the prolonged dependence of infants and small children on adults seems to be a significant consideration. This tendency carries over into sexual relationships, so that men and women tend to attach importance to the persons with whom they have sexual connection and tend to cultivate their relations with them. Associated with this is the universal tendency for males to be combative and competitive regarding sexual access to females. Finally, for a variety of reasons that are yet unclear, men and women who have grown up together as siblings tend not to establish sexual liaisons with one another.[7]

7. For recent speculation on incest and its prohibition, see Murdock (1949:284–313), Goody (1956), Slater (1959), Stephens (1963:259–265), Aberle *et al.* (1963), Wolf (1966), and Fox (1967:54–76).

A consequence of these universal human tendencies is that men and women develop continuing social relationships with two categories of persons: those with whom they are intimately associated in childhood as members of the same domestic unit, and those with whom they establish sexual liaisons as young adults. There is little overlap of these categories.

The transaction that establishes parenthood simultaneously establishes siblinghood. The sibling relationship is developed before the onset of sexual maturity of at least one of a sibling pair. A different transaction is needed to establish a continuing sexual partnership. A clear definition of rights and priorities relating to sexual access is necessary if the partnership is to be a continuing one; and both the principal parties to the partnership and other members of the community must know when the partnership, with its attendant rights and priorities, has gone into effect. Some kind of communicative act, however simple in form, is needed to signify that a change in jural relations among people—a public transaction—has occurred. The act may be no more than establishment of a common residence or unconcealed (as distinct from concealed) visitation at night.

Because rights and obligations other than those pertaining to sexual access can be vested in the sibling relationship, a definition of marriage that includes other than considerations of sex and reproduction cannot be applied universally—as long, that is, as we assume that marriage involves a transaction that links two persons in a manner they were not linked before. This has been clearly understood by Fortes, who has said (1962:8),

> Anthropologists agree that what distinguishes the conjugal relationship from all other dyadic relationships, and isolates it as the core of the domestic domain, is the exclusive, or at the minimum privileged, sexual rights and claims of the spouses on each other. These rights and claims pertain to socially responsible procreative sexuality as opposed to the irresponsible juvenile and adolescent sexual indulgence which is often condoned, if not freely allowed, pre-maritally.

I would myself define marriage, then, as a transaction and resulting contract in which a person (male or female, corporate or individual, in person or by proxy) establishes a continuing claim to the right of sexual access to a woman—this right having priority over rights of sexual access others currently have or may subsequently acquire in relation to her (except in a similar transaction) until the contract resulting from the transaction is terminated—and in which the woman involved is eligible to bear children.[8] This phrasing allows for marriages like those reported for Dahomey (Herskovits 1938 I:319-322), where a woman may marry another woman, exercising her right of sexual access and her right to sire children through someone acting in her name. It allows for the possibility of a group of brothers as a corporation taking a woman as their corporate wife, as seems to have been a practice of the Iravas of southwestern India from the account by Aiyappan (1945: 98–103). It also allows for the so-called ghost marriages of the Nuer (Evans-Pritchard 1951:109–116), in which a man takes a wife in the name of a dead brother or son for whom he acts as proxy.

The conjugal relationship established by a marriage may include many rights and privileges pertaining to other than sexual matters, but they are irrelevant to the general definition of marriage.[9] These additional rights may be acquired in the same transaction as the one in which rights of sexual access are acquired, or they may be acquired bit by bit in a series of distinct transactions. But a relationship without continuing right of sexual access is not a conjugal one, although it involves economic cooperation, living under the same roof, and so on. On the other hand, a relationship involving sexual privilege without any priority, such as obtains in Truk between all unrelated men and women who have passed puberty, is not a con-

8. Whether or not she is capable of bearing is another matter. In this respect, the definition allows for marriage with male transvestites insofar as transvestites are categorized socially or jurally as women and, as such, are deemed eligible to bear children, although they are physically incapable of bearing them.

9. Leach (1955) gives an extended list of such rights, including a monopolistic sexual one, but he concludes that the object of *sambandham* unions among the Nayar is to establish "a socially significant 'relationship of affinity' between the husband and his wife's brothers" (p. 183). By ignoring the Nayar's natural concern with sexual access to women, clearly evident in Gough's account, he infers from the Nayar case that there is no one kind of right that is "invariably established by marriage in every known society" (p. 183). As with ethnocentrism, preoccupation with anthropological constructs, such as "affinity," may lead us on occasion to misperceive what it is we are looking at.

jugal one either. Marriage in Truk comes later, when men and women acquire sexual rights in one another to the exclusion of other people. A continual sexual relationship in which the woman is ineligible to bear children is also excluded by my definition. Such is the premarital relationship of "going steady" in some groups in the United States, and such, too, is the formal, within-moiety, "lover" relationship among the Rukuba of Nigeria (Muller 1969). The post-marital "lover" relationship among the Kofyar of Nigeria is excluded, also, by virtue of the husband's continuing priority of right (Netting 1969). Among the Nayar, on the other hand, the *sambandham* relationship is a conjugal one. I know of no society in which the definition is inapplicable.

I should add, however, that my definition does not preclude the possibility that a society may allow more than one kind of transaction that meets the definition. The Nayar *tāli*-tying ceremony meets it as well as the *sambandham* union, in that the young man involved acquires a continuing and exclusive right of sexual access for a few days of the ceremonial period, and the girl is presumably now eligible to bear children although she is not physiologically capable of it. Such an interpretation stretches the definition to the limit, but it is consistent with Gough's (1961) conclusion that there are two kinds of marriage and two kinds of husband (a "ritual" kind and a "visiting" kind) among the Nayar. And it is consistent with children's using the kinship term *appan* ("father" in other castes) only in reference to their mother's *tāli*-tying partner, when they happen to know him.

More to the point are the Okrika Ijo of the Niger delta (Williamson 1962). They recognize two kinds of marriage. In one, there is a big payment of the kind usually referred to as "brideprice," a term I avoid because it connotes the purchase of a wife rather than the purchase (or actualization of a transfer) of rights. In the other, there is only a small payment to the guardian of the bride. If a small payment is made, the resulting relationship between the spouses is roughly similar to that of the *sambandham* partners among the Nayar; but if the big payment is made, the husband acquires the proprietary rights of the guardian in his wife and her children and, with them, the obligation to educate her children and set them up in business. By my definition, there is marriage in each case, but with the big payment an additional transaction has been added to the purely marital one. That the Okrika Ijo thus separate rights of sexual access from other rights and duties relating to a woman and her children, while at the same time allowing for their being brought together in a single package, further underscores the practical utility of defining marriage for comparative purposes in the way I have just done.[10]

Consider, now, the Nuer of Africa, whose marital customs have been recounted in detail by Evans-Pritchard (1951). He describes several kinds of union that may be arranged between a man and a woman. He calls such unions "marriage" when cattle are transferred from the husband and his kin to the wife's parents and kin. This transfer gives the husband important proprietary rights in the wife and in the children she shall thereafter bear, regardless of who is their actual genitor. Evans-Pritchard uses "concubinage" to refer to unions in which no payment of cattle for proprietary rights in the woman and her offspring has been made. A man may pay cattle to obtain proprietary rights in a child he has sired by a "concubine," but this does not give him proprietary rights in her nor in her other children, even those sired by him. "Concubinage" may be converted into "marriage" on the full payment of cattle by the man and his kin to the woman's parents and kin.

What Evans-Pritchard calls a "concubine," then, is a woman who has freely entered into a private arrangement with a man without involving his or her kin. Either partner can terminate it readily, since no property is involved and proprietary rights in the children re-

---

10. It has been traditional among anthropologists to distinguish between rights *in uxorem* (rights in a woman as wife) and rights *in genetricem* (rights in a woman as bearer of children and in her children). As we shall see below in connection with parenthood, however, the distinction does not exactly fit the Okrika Ijo situation. A man has rights in both the woman and her children in both the big-payment and little-payment marriages, but in the latter these rights are severely limited and what I am calling proprietary rights are acquired only in the former. Buchler and Selby (1968:29) suggest that ". . . on a cross-cultural basis an intensity order or rank ordering of ordinal or greater than ordinal strength of the transference of these rights [*in uxorem* and *in genetricem*] would enable us to provide a somewhat more contextually relevant basis for formulating a typology of family forms than is available at present." I agree in principle, but suspect that it will require something conceptually more sophisticated thtan the simple dichotomy implied by *in uxorem* and *in genetricem*.

main with the woman's father or guardian. Evans-Pritchard says
that in daily life it is not possible for an observer to tell "concubines"
from "married women" in Nuer households. The difference is not in
the conduct of domestic life, but in the allocation of jural rights in
the relationship. By my definition, we have, as among the Ijo, two
forms of marriage, one a contract involving a transfer of proprietary
rights and the other a contract in which proprietary rights are not
involved.

In this distinction lies a major difficulty in formulating a general
definition of marriage for comparative purposes. Among the Nayar,
we saw, there is no transfer of proprietary rights in a woman and
her children from one party (individual or corporation) to another.
Among the Ijo and Nuer, it is possible to have unions accompanied
by such transfer and unions not so accompanied. For such a transfer
to occur, there must be a transaction between whoever is the current
holder of these rights and whoever is to acquire them. The transaction is not one that the bride and groom are free to make on their
own. But when proprietary rights are not being transferred, then a
man and woman can enter into an arrangement regarding matters in
their personal control without the consent of guardians and kin.

We recognize this in the United States. If the bride is not legally
adult, she may not marry without her guardian's consent. But when
she becomes adult, her parents and guardian lose their proprietary
rights in her person. She is then free to live her own life and to
negotiate her own marriage as she wishes. Her parents no longer
have jural authority over her nor jural responsibility for her. We
happen to accord husband and wife considerable rights in one another and in their preadult children; but they do not get them
because these rights were transferred to them from their parents.
After becoming adult, they remain answerable for some things to
the community as legally represented in the institutions of state and
church. The state and, when appropriate, the church are the authorities that guarantee a husband and wife their rights in one another,
subject to certain conditions.[11] Unions to which the state or church

11. The concern of the state may be no more than to have a record of the
fact that a man and a woman have agreed to be married. The State of
Pennsylvania, for example, explicitly recognizes as a legal marriage a union
in which the couple marry themselves without a minister or justice of the

have not been a party are not recognized and hence not guaranteed or respected by them. Unions not sanctioned by the state are unions by private agreement involving only those matters over which the consenting parties have direct control: sexual access and cohabitation. Since the state was not a party to the contract, it need not be a party to its termination.

In culturally plural societies, the crown or state may recognize one cultural system of jural relationship, while subgroups within the total polity develop or preserve folk cultures with different systems of jural relationships. What is under private control by the conventions of a folk culture may not be under private control according to the rules of the state culture, and the state may not recognize forms of guardianship and proprietary right that are recognized in a folk culture. The same arrangement might meet my definition of marriage in one and not meet it in the other. When such occurs, the larger political entity is an appropriate unit for cross-cultural comparison only with respect to its official state culture. The separate folk cultures carried by communities within it—ethnic communities, regional communities, or social classes—must be treated independently as separate units of cultural comparison.

FAMILY

In discussion so far our attention has been on rights, privileges, and duties—on the jural aspects of social relations. My concern has been with these as they relate to the handling of problems of social living that arise from human nature: from human sexuality, from the human tendency to develop strong affective ties, from the long dependence of children on adults, and from the tendency to avoid sexual

---

peace. The state issues a marriage license form for such a "common-law" marriage, known in Philadelphia as a "Quaker marriage license." The license makes no provision for a marrying authority other than the bride and groom, who sign the license instead of a minister or justice as the officiating authority. The added signatures of two witnesses and deposition of the signed form with the appropriate government office puts the consensual union on record as a marriage having the same jural status as any other properly recorded marriage. One need not be a member of the Society of Friends to use this marriage license. What is derogated as a "common-law" marriage elsewhere has acquired social respectability and official recognition because of the social standing of the Society of Friends in Pennsylvania.

liaisons with siblings. We observed that siblings and sex partners are two distinct categories that rarely overlap, with adults tending to have strong affective ties in two directions. I must now add some other considerations arising from human nature and affecting the nature and distribution of rights and duties. They are the universal tendency to a division of labor by sex and the universal tendency to male dominance over women and children.[12]

The division of labor by sex makes it necessary for men and women to cooperate economically, and it makes both sexes indispensable in the maintenance, socialization, and education of children, as anthropologists have often observed (e.g., Murdock 1949:7–8). The traditional view in anthropology, we saw, has been to attribute economic cooperation and responsibility for maintaining, socializing, and educating children to the conjugal relationship as among its universal attributes. But it is apparent that they are vested in the brother-sister relationship among the Nayar; and they are largely vested in the brother-sister or some close consanguineal relationship in the small-payment marriages among the Okrika Ijo. Indeed, we can see the Nayar as representing an extreme in which brothers and sisters turn to one another for virtually everything except sexual gratification, only the latter being sought in the conjugal relationship. Our own middle-class culture is close to the opposite extreme, with adult men and women expected to turn to their sex partners for virtually everything and to their siblings for very little. Thus nearly all the privileges, rights, and responsibilities that we associate with the positions of husband and father in our society are associated with the positions of brother and maternal uncle among the Nayar, and with the former or latter positions among the Okrika Ijo according to the form of marriage contracted.

These considerations lead me to concur with Adams (1960), Bohannan (1963:73), and Fox (1967:39–40) that a woman and her dependent children represent the nuclear familial group in human societies. When the woman's sexual partner is added to this group in a functionally significant way, the result is an elementary conjugal family (Murdock's nuclear family). When the woman's

12. For a discussion of male dominance and its possible relation to human evolution and sexual behavior, see Fox (1968). For the difference it makes between patrilineal and matrilineal descent groups, see Schneider (1961).

brothers (and other close consanguines) are added to the mother-children group in a functionally significant way, the result is what Linton (1936:154–163) called a consanguine family. What the particular functions are is irrelevant. Levy and Fallers (1959) have defined the family as the group, conjugal or consanguine, that is primarily responsible for the socialization of children. I prefer to define the family as a woman and her dependent children plus whomever else they are joined to through marriage or consanguinity in a minimal functioning group, whatever the group's functions may be. Because dependent children are included, socialization is very likely to be a function of such a group.

According to what I have given as definitions of marriage and the family, it is not possible to have a conjugal family without marriage, but it is quite possible to have marriage without a conjugal family. The Nayar are a case in point. They have consanguine families but lack elementary conjugal families. Middle-class Americans, by contrast, have elementary conjugal families but lack consanguine families. The people of Truk have both conjugal and consanguine families, having a division of functions between a woman's husband and her brothers in relation to herself and her children. Many of the world's societies are like Truk in this respect, both husband and brother being significantly attached to a woman and her children at the same time, but in different ways. The Okrika Ijo represent the fourth possible arrangement, where a woman and her children may be attached significantly to her husband or to her brother (or other consanguineal guardian), but not to both at the same time. Here the conjugal and consanguine families are recognized alternatives.

All the foregoing considerations help, I think, to clarify the problem of marriage and family organization in the Caribbean area, where the so-called matrifocal family has been an object of considerable discussion (Smith 1956, 1962; Cohen 1956; Clarke 1957; Adams 1960; Davenport 1961; Otterbein 1965; Goode 1966). Here, as among the Okrika Ijo, we seem to have various forms of family organization, ranging from almost completely consanguine to almost completely conjugal ones.

Davenport (1961) describes such a state of affairs for the lower classes in Jamaica. There, as elsewhere in the Caribbean, matters appear confused, because only one form of marriage is recognized by the middle and upper classes. The lower classes, however, distinguish between a union corresponding to the one recognized in law and by the middle and upper classes (one they too call "marriage") and unions they refer to as "living a sweetheart life" or "common-law" marriage," often referred to by social scientists and administrative authorities as consensual unions. The stability of many of these consensual unions, however, and the clearly understood customary rights and duties of the participants indicate that in Jamaican lower-class culture, they are a form of marriage according to my definition, whether or not they are recognized as such by the courts and governing authorities. This is not altered by the ease with which these unions are terminated nor by the very short duration of many of them. The officially preferred marriage is regularly associated with the conjugal family, whereas the nonlegal or common-law marriage, Davenport shows, is variously associated with either the conjugal or the consanguine family, depending on economic and other considerations.

This example calls attention to the distinctions made by some authorities (e.g., Winch 1968:2), who use "common-law marriage" to refer to a union recognized by statute law or by judicial precedent (as in the United Kingdom and United States) or by state or colonial authority in relation to subject populations with their own customary law or *adat* (as in Moslem countries and Indonesia), and who use "consensual union," as in the Caribbean, to refer to a union that is not recognized in the state's courts. In plural societies, statute law and the state courts reflect the values and social customs of the ruling classes or ethnic groups, who tend to take a superior attitude toward the customary practices of the relatively powerless classes and ethnic groups. Gloria Marshall (1968:9) has said that "where marriage is defined by the state, it is possible to describe most of its jural entailments by reference to one or more legal codes adopted by the state," but "among many of the peoples studied by anthropologists, the jural tenets governing marriage cannot be ascertained by reference to codes laid down by a state and hence must be derived from the study of recurrent patterns of behavior and of folk models that prescribe ideal behavior." Thus she accords the customs of stateless societies the status of being jural but denies it to the customs of lower-class groups and ethnic minorities within states, a procedure that is methodologically impermissable for controlled comparative study. That the customs of the upper classes may be regarded as better than the customs of the lower classes, even by members of the lower classes, is no different from the attitude of many Melanesians today that their traditional customs are "bad" by comparison with the ways of their European rulers, which are "good" and to be emulated, as in the case of the Paliau Movement in the Admiralty Islands, described by Mead (1956) and Schwartz (1962). In culturally plural societies, cultures get ranked according to preference ratings. This does not make the rules of one culture any less jural than the rules of another for those who happen to play by that particular set of rules.

The short duration of many conjugal unions in Jamaica calls our attention to something else. My definition of marriage does not imply that the union be permanent or even of long duration, only that the husband's right of sexual access be continuing and take priority over the rights others may have in the wife until the union is terminated. Other transactions or agreements may occur subsequently and create a stronger bond between the married pair, making the union more difficult to dissolve and more permanent. But as I have shown, a generally applicable definition of marriage can be phrased only with reference to rights of sexual access. By my definition, we cannot properly say that some couples are more married than others; but we can say that some couples are more committed in their marriage than others, or more bound by duties to outside interested parties, and that some marriages are more durable or more freighted with responsibility than others. Thus Evans-Pritchard (1951:108) says that "the Nuer do not consider the union to be complete till a child is born to it." But he does not say they are not married until a child is born. Some societies may allow for a gradient from marriages that are minimally freighted and most readily terminated—even regarded as strictly tentative by the participants—to marriages that are heavily freighted and looked upon as permanent. Lower-class marriages in the Caribbean would appear to provide just such a gradient.

PARENTHOOD

The Okrika Ijo, Nuer, and lower-class Jamaicans may be similar in having more than one kind of marriage, but they differ in the kinds of proprietary rights men have in women and children. This difference brings me back to the second universal tendency I mentioned above: the tendency to male dominance over women and children. This tendency gives men a proprietary interest in the sexuality of women and in the labor and services that women and children can provide. Men tend to treat these things as a form of property.

Proprietary rights in the sexuality and labor of a woman and her children may be vested in the husband and father or in the brother and maternal uncle. The allocation of these rights also relates to the distinction between the conjugal and consanguine forms of the family. But like other forms of property, they can be subject to inheritance, sale, gift, loan, rental—whatever kinds of transactions and transfers of title a society's rules of property allow. The Okrika Ijo illustrate this well. Elaborate trafficking in the sexuality of women is reported for the Rukuba (Muller 1969) and Irigwe (Sangree 1969) of Nigeria. The widespread practice of various forms of adoption and fosterage indicate how common are transactions in the rights of parenthood.[13]

Failure to take proper account of the transactional nature of social relationships—especially in their jural aspects, where rights and duties are involved[14]—may well have contributed to anthropology's conceptual problems in defining marriage, family, and kinship. It is in connection with parenthood—fatherhood, especially—that problems arise here.

Consideration of the family inevitably leads to consideration of parenthood, and consideration of parenthood is obviously the key to any cross-culturally useful definition of kinship, as Malinowski

13. For an analysis of adoption and fosterage, see my account in Carroll (1970). See also Goody (1969).

14. Drawing on the concepts of Hohfeld (1919), I define a jural relationship as one in which one party—be it an individual, a group, or the community—can make a demand upon another party, and there is public agreement that the other is obligated to comply with the demand. Such agreement as to demand-right and duty may derive from oral tradition (as with customary law), from written or unwritten contractual arrangement, from written or oral decree by a recognized authority, or from a precedent-making judicial decision (written or unwritten). I regard the nature of the sanction system by which publicly agreed-upon rights are enforced to be irrelevant to the definition of jural relationships. The existence of jural relationships and the effectiveness of institutional machinery to administer them are related but different matters.

(1930:146) clearly saw. In spite of all the anthropological discussion and debate regarding kinship and its analysis, it remains an undefined concept. We assume we know what kinship is and go on from there. Or we define it tautologically in terms of consanguinity or descent (e.g., Radcliffe-Brown 1950:4; Eggan 1968:390). But consanguinity and descent bring us back to parenthood. We anthropologists have distinguished between what we have called biological and sociological parenthood, but we have not yet seriously tried to define sociological parenthood for cross-cultural purposes, other than to say that it involves rights and duties (e.g., Barnes 1958) and to link it to marriage (Malinowski 1930). Until we have a workable definition, the concept of kinship must remain imprecise; for kinship, at least consanguineal kinship, derives from a chain of socially recognized parent-child connections.[15]

Defining parenthood for comparative purposes is not easy. I need only call attention to the assertions in the literature that the Australian aborigines ignore biological paternity as a basis for recognizing fatherhood (mistakenly construed by most early theorists as primitive ignorance). There is the anthropologically famous case of the Trobriand Islanders, who say that sexual intercourse is necessary at least once so that a woman's womb will be opened to entry by a spirit of her clan, whose union with her menstrual blood results in her pregnancy, and who also assert as a dogma that men have nothing to do otherwise with the begetting of children (Malinowski 1929).[16] Similar beliefs are reported for the Pacific island

15. There has been some argument regarding the nature of kinship, reviewed by Schneider (1964). Clearly what defines kinship as such is not the content of kin relationships, but the fact that the relationships, whatever their content, are based on a socially recognized chain of childbearing and child-begetting. The chain itself is a natural phenomenon, but all societies make something of it culturally. What they make of it is necessarily related to the pattern of dependence of human infants and children on their nurturing adults and everything that follows from it. In this respect, Schneider is right in arguing that kin relationships have a content that, in part at least, is distinctive from the content of other social relationships.

16. In an unpublished work, Powell (n.d.) reports that the Trobriand people have two versions of the male role in procreation, one as reported by Malinowski, which has to do with jural matters, and another in which male sperm is also said to be a part of what joins with the menstrual blood to form a baby, this version being used in informal contexts where jural rights are not at issue. Powell agrees with Malinowski that for jural purposes a man's rights in his children derive from his being their mother's husband and not from his being their genitor.

of Yap (Schneider 1962, 1968c). We are so used to thinking of parenthood in procreative terms that we easily forget that the acts of begetting and bearing children may not in themselves entitle men or women to any rights and privileges relating to children. But I do not imply by this that procreation is entirely irrelevant to the definition of parenthood, either.

We begin with motherhood and observe that in many societies not all women are eligible to bear children. In our own society, for example, a woman is considered ineligible to bear children if she is not married. Women who are classed as *nikiranroro* in the southern Gilbert Islands are eligible to have sexual relations with men but ineligible to bear children, abortion being the means of birth control. In Truk, on the other hand, a woman is eligible simply by being old enough to conceive. In societies where eligibility is an important consideration, a woman may not be allowed any rights in her children if she is considered ineligible to have them, or if she conceived in an improper sexual union. Legitimacy may not serve as a criterion for a cross-cultural definition of marriage, but it is clearly relevant to a definition of motherhood.

By motherhood, then, we are talking not simply about a biological connection between a woman and a child, but about other kinds of connection or relationship as well. In addition to biological or natural motherhood, there is psychic motherhood. As far as I know, all peoples have an idealized affective relationship that is supposed to develop between a child and the woman who is its principal nurturer. It may or may not be rationalized as deriving from a maternal "instinct" or from something inherent in a "blood tie." Beyond psychic motherhood, there is jural motherhood, consisting of rights and duties in relation to a child. The matter of eligibility, to which I referred, for example, has to do with jural motherhood; and it is with jural motherhood that I am concerned here.

If we try to define jural motherhood by the kinds of rights and duties comprising it, we are in trouble, as the societies we have already considered reveal. For the ways in which rights in children distribute socially and the very content of the rights themselves vary considerably cross-culturally. We are dealing with a jural role, then, but can identify it cross-culturally not by its content but by some constant among the criteria by which people are entitled to the role.

My suggested definition of marriage provides one such constant. A more immediately relevant constant is the fact that children are borne by women and, until very recently in human history, are dependent on the women who bear them for their survival during their first year of life. In these and perhaps other ways, as well, the nature of our species provides conditions that favor the close association of women and the children they bear. Psychic motherhood is a product of this association. Women and their associated children live in groups with other women, and for this reason each woman's association with the children she has borne must be recognized and subjected to regulation of some kind. Her rights as distinct from the rights of adult women generally and as distinct from the rights of adult men need to be understood by all.

With the foregoing in mind, we may say that jural motherhood consists of the rights and duties a woman has claim to in relation to a child by virtue of her having borne it, provided she is eligible to bear it and provided no other disqualifying circumstances attend its birth. Her being married may or may not affect her eligibility; and if she is married, her husband's acceptance of the child may or may not be a consideration. The rights and duties vary cross-culturally, but there is no functioning society in which otherwise qualified women are without rights of some kind in the children they bear. These rights may be delegated to other women in fosterage, they may be transferred outright to someone else in adoption, or they may be surrendered in the event of divorce. It is evident, nevertheless, that where adoption is allowed, the rights of the adopting mother are based on the rights that women who are eligible to bear children are understood to have in the children they bear.

Fatherhood, as I have already implied, is not as straightforward a matter. The Tiwi of Melville Island, Australia, as described by Jane Goodale (1959, 1962), illustrate some of the problems.

Among the Tiwi, when a girl reaches menarche, she enters into a lifelong relationship with a man or youth. The man has the responsibility of supplying her with game, and in return he has sexual and economic rights in any daughters the young lady may ever bear; but he has no sexual or economic rights in the young lady herself. She is, in effect, what we would call his mother-in-law, and her future daughters are his wives. He dreams the names of the children these as yet unborn wives will someday bear. For ritual purposes they will be his children. In the meantime he inherits sexual rights in women in whom his paternal grandfather and older brothers had rights, inheriting their mothers as his mothers-in-law, so he does not necessarily lack for wives while he waits. A man may continue to acquire mothers-in-law throughout his life. If he does, he is not likely to live to see the birth of all his wives. His younger brothers and sons' sons inherit his rights.

When a girl is about eight years old, she is sent to her husband—the man who is her mother's son-in-law—to join his household. It will already include the wives he has inherited from his father's father or older brothers and may include a wife he has stolen from another man and for whom he subsequently paid compensation. The little girl is trained by these older women in her domestic duties, and when she reaches a suitable age, she is initiated into sex by her considerably older husband. At menarche, she in turn acquires a son-in-law, designated by her mother's original husband or by whoever has now succeeded to his paternal rights in her person. The children she bears will receive the names her original husband (her mother's son-in-law) or his legitimate successor has dreamed for them. By the time she bears them, however, she may no longer be a member of her original husband's household. He may have died, in which case she will have joined the household of his younger brother or of his son's son by a much older wife. Or she may be living with a man with whom she eloped and who, by paying her original husband compensation, acquired sexual and economic rights in her person. But her original husband, or his heir, is still her mother's son-in-law and still the man who dreamed whatever children she may ever bear. Her current husband must help provide for her children's economic welfare and can demand their economic cooperation as members of his household; but if he was not eligible to dream them, it appears, he has no rights in them of a ritual nature, although he may perform some ritual duties relating to them. In matters of everyday living, the children refer to their mother's current husband by the kinship term we translate as 'father.' But on ritual occasions, they refer to their mother's son-in-law (or to whoever has inherited his rights) as their 'father.'

Thus the Tiwi draw a sharp distinction between the rights and duties a man has in relation to children of women in his household

—women in whom he has current sexual and economic rights—and the rights he has in the children of his mother-in-law's daughters—the women in whom he has original sexual and economic rights (or in whom he has inherited these rights). Furthermore, although the Tiwi are often well aware who a child's natural father is, a man has absolutely no rights in a child simply by virtue of being its genitor.[17] He may assume minor duties, but he is not obligated to do so. Physical paternity is irrelevant to jural fatherhood among the Tiwi. Being the mother's husband, however, is very relevant indeed. What complicates the picture is that there are two senses in which a man can be the mother's husband. He can be the son-in-law of the mother's mother and hence the mother's first husband; or he can be a subsequent husband of the mother. A subsequent husband who is not the heir of the first husband has fewer rights in his wife's children than a first husband has. There are two kinds of marriage, and each produces a different kind of jural fatherhood.

The Lozi of Zambia provide an antithetical picture. Gluckman (1950:187) is explicit that "under Lozi law the pater is the genitor, not the mother's husband." A man who has begotten a child by another man's wife may claim the child. At the same time, marriage becomes jurally effective on the groom's making the marriage payment to the bride's parents, and the "marriage payment gives a man the right to exclude other men from his wife, and the right to control her" (p. 186).

In societies where a man has jural rights in the children he begets, there is necessarily a heightened concern to limit sexual access to women in order to be reasonably certain of who a child's genitor is. A husband's exclusive right of sexual access makes him the presumed genitor. The burden of proof that another is indeed the genitor rests on the claimant when children are born out of wed-

17. Barnes (1961, 1964) has called attention to the necessity of distinguishing between the physical begetter and bearer in an absolute biological sense (the genetic father and mother) and the begetter and bearer as defined by local cultural ideas (the genitor and genetrix). The distinction has been supported by Buchler (1966). It refines the traditional anthropological dichotomy between genitor and pater (jural father). When I speak here of the rights or other interests of the genitor and genetrix, I am necessarily speaking of the natural parents as culturally defined. Only culturally defined entities can have any kind of social recognition, jural or otherwise.

lock. The Rukuba of Nigeria (Muller 1969) are especially revealing in this matter. A Rukuba woman may be and often is married to two or more men at the same time, each husband belonging to a different patrilineal clan or subclan. She may reside with only one husband at a time; and once she takes up residence with one, she may not leave him to reside with another husband until a full year has elapsed. If she then moves, she must remain with the next husband for at least a year before she can move back to the first or on to yet another husband. By means of the one-year rule, the Rukuba keep biological paternity reasonably clear. The cohabiting husband has exclusive sexual right for as long as his wife is residing with him and is the presumed genitor of any child his wife bears that results from a pregnancy begun while she was residing with him.

Jural fatherhood, then, whether it belongs to the genitor or to the mother's husband, derives from the marital relationship, which in every society provides the prototypic situation for the definition of whatever rights men have in children as participants in their procreation. In any society, however, there are bound to be occasions when a child's begetter is other than the mother's husband. When the two do not coincide as they ideally should, some cultures accord jural fatherhood, as defined in the prototypic context of marriage, to the mother's husband, others accord it to the genitor (if his identity is established), and others break it down, granting some of its rights and duties to the genitor and some to the mother's husband. These different approaches are clearly seen in situations where the mother has been physically separated from her husband for a considerable period prior to her pregnancy. They are also evident in divorce and remarriage. But in those situations where the mother's husband and the probable genitor are not the same person, what is understood to be jural fatherhood or a modified form of it regularly derives from the rights and duties that the mother's husband enjoys when he is also presumed to be the genitor.

With the foregoing in mind, then, I would suggest as a working definition that jural fatherhood consists of the rights and duties in relation to a child a person has claim to by virtue of his being married at the onset of her pregnancy to the woman who bore it, provided he is otherwise eligible and provided no disqualifying circumstances attend the child's birth. The same rights, or a reduced

version of them, may be claimable in some societies by the acknowledged genitor other than the mother's husband or by the mother's
subsequent husband. Not being the genitor may or may not be a
disqualifying condition. Ceasing to be the mother's husband may
or may not be a disqualifying condition. The rights and duties of
fatherhood, as thus defined, may be very few; and they may even
approach the vanishing point, as among the Nayar.[18] Nevertheless,
the only cross-cultural constant that provides a point of departure
for systematic comparative study is provided by marriage and the
jural relationship of a man to the children a woman conceives while
he is married to her.

Kinship, I have said, cannot be defined without reference to
parent-child relationships. Jural, as distinct from biological, kinship
consists of the father-child and mother-child relationships, as jurally
defined, and any other jural relationships that depend for their
definition on the genealogical proliferation of jurally defined
parent-child and husband-wife ties. Kin relationships can, therefore, be described as relative products of "parent," "child," and
"spouse," together with whatever indications of age and sex may
also be required in specific cases, as with the kintype notation used
by anthropologists.[19] An uncle among ourselves, for example, may
be described as a parent's parent's male child or a parent's parent's

---

18. Like the Tiwi, the Nayar have two kinds of marriage, as I indicated
above, and thus two kinds of fatherhood. There is the ritual fatherhood of the
tāli-tier, who has the right to be called *appan* ("father") and who is entitled
to mortuary observances by the children his ritual wife bears. There is the
secular fatherhood of the *sambandham* partner who acknowledges paternity
and legitimizes the child's status in Nayar society. Thus my interpretation
differs from Buchler and Selby's (1968:28–29), who speak only of the ritual
father as the "father" in Nayar culture. The one kind of father has almost
no rights in the child, and the other has none at all although he has the duty
to legitimize. But in each case fatherhood consists of whatever rights and/or
duties pertain to the mother's husband, the one ritual and the other secular.

19. Buchler and Selby (1968:35) have properly observed that the kin types
we designate by the anthropological notation F (father), M (mother), B
(brother), MB (mother's brother), etc., are "sociological constructs, based in
part upon biological considerations." I would add that for any particular
society to which we apply them, they have meaning according to the cultural
definition of jural parenthood in that society. The definitions of kin types
that comprise a genealogy in one culture are not necessarily those that
comprise it in the next; but the general definitions of fatherhood and motherhood I have given here show us how to arrive at these different cultural
definitions in each case.

female child's spouse. Exact genealogical connection between ego and alter need not be known, provided they can establish a kinsman in common from whom genealogical reckoning can then be made to either ego or alter. Thus, if A is my cousin and your uncle, then you are my cousin by common American reckoning. So-called fictive kin relationships are ones that are accorded the jural content of genealogically constituted kin relationships and by analogy are linguistically designated accordingly.

This seems so obvious that I would not mention it at all, except that the definition of kinship has been a problem in the history of anthropology. Most recently, for example, Scheffler (1970) has taken issue with the old argument put forth by Rivers (1924:52–53) that kinship is a purely social relationship based on genealogy, which cannot be understood or defined in terms of consanguinity (by which he meant biological kinship). Rivers was, of course, talking of jural kinship; and by overstating the case, he ended with a half truth. Scheffler rests his argument, as anyone must, on the criteria of parenthood, but he derives jural parenthood directly from biological parenthood. This leads him to differ, also, with Radcliffe-Brown (1950), who said that marriage determines jural, or what he called social, fatherhood, a position also taken by Malinowski (1930). Radcliffe-Brown, too, overstates the case by implying that marriage *determines* fatherhood. The Lozi make clear that it need not. On the other hand, the Tiwi make it equally clear that biological fatherhood need not determine jural fatherhood either. Scheffler correctly insists that what we recognize as jural kinship and parenthood in our own and other societies rests ultimately on a relationship involving biological procreation. But this anchoring relationship is that of the natural mother and her child, not the natural father and his child. Natural fatherhood can be reasonably inferred only in social arrangements in which men have close to exclusive rights of continuing sexual access to women, in arrangements of the kind I have called marriage.

To say this is not to imply that marriage determines jural fatherhood or kinship in the rules of any particular culture. Rather, it is to recognize that fatherhood and kinship through males are *derived* from marriage, no matter what the rules and ideology are—are derived from the fact that in all societies procreation takes place in the context of regulations that severely restrict the sexual access of males to females of childbearing age. If jural fatherhood is allocated culturally to the mother's husband, then jural kinship through males is reckoned through a chain of mothers' husbands. If jural father-hood is allocated in the genitor rather than to the mother's husband, then kinship is reckoned through a chain of presumed genitors. If the rights of jural fatherhood are divided between genitor and mother's husband, jural kinship may be reckoned through either or through both at once. In the United States, for example, adoption transfers jural kinship from the kinsmen of the genitor to the kins-men of the adopting father; but in Truk adoption only suspends the jural kinship of the original father's kinsmen during the time the child is a minor, for jural parenthood and not jural kinship is all that is transferred in the adoption transaction. The adopted child acquires an additional set of kinsmen without losing the original set. But we know what jural fatherhood is and what kinship through males is in both societies by starting with the relationships of men with the children their wives bear.

Beyond kinship *per se* is the much discussed subject of organized social groups in which membership involves considerations of kin-ship. I shall deal with it at length in Chapter 2. But I cannot consider fatherhood among the Okrika Ijo without some reference to it.

As described by Williamson (1962), the Ijo of Okrika, Nigeria, are organized into kin-based corporations or "houses," which can claim the undivided loyalty of their members. There are several different arrangements by which men and women may establish continuing sexual liaisons or marriages. As I have already indicated, the two most important ones differ in the size of the payment to the woman's guardian. With a big payment, the husband acquires com-plete control of his wife's sexuality and her economic services. He can as her new guardian subsequently give her out in a small-payment marriage to someone else. He is responsible for the education of any children his wife may bear and for equipping them with the tools of their trades. He must finance his wife's daughters' puberty ceremonies, and by doing so he acquires control of their sexuality as well. His house can claim all the wife's children as members, regardless of genitor. A woman cannot ever enter into more than one marriage involving a big payment. She can be "separated" from her big-payment husband and married to someone else in a little-payment marriage, but she cannot be divorced from her big-payment husband's authority over herself and her children. If a small payment is made, the husband acquires sexual privileges and the right to economic services attendant on cohabitation, but the wife remains a member of her former house and may even continue to reside there. The marriage is easily terminated. All the rights and duties relating to the wife's children I have just described rest not with the husband but with whatever man financed the wife's puberty ceremony or with whoever subsequently acquired those rights from him. He makes the payments for her son's wives, and he collects the payments from her daughter's husbands. A small-payment husband has a sentimental interest in his children, does things for them, gives them presents, and may be much loved by them in return, but his rights and duties are minimal.

When there was strong competition in fishing and trading among the different houses, the Okrika Ijo preferred to acquire wives for their men in big-payment marriages in order to get control of the children. At the same time, they preferred to give their daughters and sisters in small-payment marriages in order to retain control of the children. Under polygyny, which was widespread, they engineered this having their cake and eating it by acquiring wives from the neighboring Ibo people under big-payment arrangements and establishing liaisons among themselves largely in small-payment marriages.

The Okrika Ijo thus distinguish the proprietary rights a man (and through him his house) may have in the sexuality, labor, and loyalty of a woman and her children from the rights he may have as a woman's continuing sex partner—her husband. A man acquires the proprietary rights by financing a woman's puberty ceremony. These rights may be inherited by his younger brother, his sister's son, or his own son, provided (I infer) that the heir is a member of the former holder's house—in other words, by his nearest junior male kinsman who is also a member of his house. But the proprietary rights may be transferred in full to the woman's husband, who must make a big-payment marriage to acquire them. In a small-payment marriage, on the other hand, the proprietary rights are not transferred to the husband, who obtains only concubicular and minor cohabitational privileges. The principal duties of maintenance, education, and sponsorship of the woman's children lie with whoever has the proprietary rights in them, not necessarily with their mother's husband.

What, then, is fatherhood among the Okrika Ijo? My first conclusion was that by my definition there are two forms of fatherhood among them, one with and one without proprietary rights, just as there are two forms of fatherhood among the Tiwi. Reflection led me to change my mind. For an Ijo man's claim to proprietary rights in a woman's children does not depend on his being married to the woman—on his being her recognized sex partner at the time of her pregnancy and parturition. The rights a man can claim in his wife's children simply by virtue of being her husband (and their presumed genitor) are the ones associated with small-payment marriage. They are also present in big-payment marriages but are overshadowed there by the proprietary rights. In many cultures, the rights that go with fatherhood include the proprietary rights in children, but in Okrika Ijo culture they do not, although fathers may acquire them and even prefer to do so.

How the ethnocentric assumption that proprietary rights in children accompany fatherhood and result from marriage may bias ethnographic description is illustrated by an account of the Efik by Simmons (1960). The Efik are neighbors of the Ijo, and they appear to have rather similar customs relating to marriage, marriage payments, and proprietary rights. But Simmons saw only unions with the pig payment as marriage and referred to the others as consensual unions outside of marriage. He was free to do so, of course. But his account suggests that he saw the big-payment union as the true equivalent or analogue of our marriage, as the union fitting the idea that jural fatherhood involves proprietary rights and that marriage is what bestows them, and therefore as the only union among the Efik worthy of being called marriage for comparative purposes. Thus unconsciously and unwittingly we prejudice our understanding of the things we study.

How much so becomes clear when we consider the principles of house membership among the Ijo. If we follow Simmons and apply his definitions for the Efik to the Ijo, limiting marriage and jural fatherhood to big-payment unions, it follows that a child belongs to his father's (mother's big-payment husband's) house, provided he has a jural father. Otherwise, when his mother is not married (in the big-payment sense) and he has no father, he belongs to his mother's house. This view might lead us to regard membership in Ijo houses as properly deriving from father-child ties. Thus we would overlook the simple rule that a child always belongs to the house of which his mother is a member at the time of his birth. By this rule, birthright membership in a house derives from the mother-child tie, an adult woman's membership being subject to change, should her husband acquire the proprietary rights in her fertility and economic services.

I could, of course, have defined fatherhood as consisting of the major set of proprietary rights a society's culture allows a man to have in a child. By this definition, we would have to say that fatherhood is sometimes the property of the mother's brother (or other consanguineal kinsman) and sometimes the property of the mother's husband (or ex-husband) among the Okrika Ijo; and we would have to say that it is regularly the property of the mother's brother among the Nayar. To compare societies according to their rules governing the possession of major proprietary rights in children is, of course, a legitimate undertaking. One can call the major bundle of rights fatherhood, if one wishes. To do so is to take the jural freight carried by what we regard as fatherhood in our own society—the *potestas*—and make it the criterion for a cross-cultural concept of fatherhood.[20]

There are obviously many different kinds of rights that a man may have in a child: rights to assistance in work, to political support, to obedience, to physical custody, to demonstrations of affection, to maintenance in old age, and so on and on. And there are also many different types of categorical relationships in which a man holding any combination of these rights may stand to a child: genitor, mother's husband, household head, mother's brother, legal guardian, ritual sponsor, and so on. I could have defined jural fatherhood as consisting of whatever rights a man may claim in a child by virtue of being its genitor, its household head, its legal

20. This Malinowski (1930) was clearly unwilling to do.

guardian, or its mother's brother, for that matter. Because we are accustomed to associate fatherhood with a man's relations to children by virtue of marriage, however, I chose to define fatherhood with reference to that universal institution. In this respect it is an appropriate definition, in keeping with anthropological tradition.

For analytical purposes, too, I think my definitions of parenthood have some utility. To illustrate this, we may consider the problem of what we mean by the adoption and fosterage of children, especially for purposes of cross-cultural comparison.

When we speak of adoption and fosterage, what we seem to have in mind is some kind of transaction. Rights in children are surrendered by one party to another in adoption; and in fosterage they are delegated by one party to another without being surrendered. We also take for granted that the rights in question, if we are talking about parental adoption, are those that were first held by the woman who bore the child and by the man who was her husband when she bore it. In other words, the rights to which a man and woman have claim in my definition of fatherhood and motherhood are what we have in mind.

I cannot leave this subject without reference to the people of Mota in the Banks Islands in Melanesia. According to the account of Rivers (1914 I:50–55) and an analysis of it by Scheffler (1970), when a Motan woman bears a child, her current husband has first claim to a major set of rights, including important proprietary rights, in the child. These rights constitute fatherhood in Motan culture, both according to Rivers and Scheffler and according to the definition of fatherhood I have offered here. The woman who bore the child also has claim to important rights in it by virtue of her having borne it. But neither she nor her husband can assert their claims until her husband has validated them by paying the midwife's fee. By doing this, the husband actually takes legal posession of the father's rights for himself and of the mother's rights for his wife in the child. If he fails or is unable to pay the midwife, the parental rights can be acquired by others. Another man can step in and pay the midwife instead. He thereby acquires the rights of fatherhood and motherhood for himself and his own wife. The husband of the woman who bore the child, however, still has a prior claim and can redeem his rights in the child by reimbursing the man who paid the midwife with 100 per cent interest. Rivers and Scheffler have referred to another man's acquisition of parental rights by paying the midwife's fee as an example of adoption. Such it can be considered when the couple with first claim agree to allow another person to take the child and prearrange for that other person to pay the midwife, whereby he legally establishes his right to take the child to his own home when it is old enough to be weaned. But Rivers reports how a wealthy man in want of a child might rush to the home of a poor man whose wife had just given birth and pay the midwife ahead of him, thereby snatching away the parental rights in the child. Here there is no agreement to transfer parental rights; there is only a taking advantage of the rules of the game.

But it is not my intention to get into the question of adoption *per se*. I mention the Mota case, because it reveals why I have been careful to define motherhood and fatherhood as rights in a child to which a woman and a man have claim, rather than rights they automatically acquire, the woman by virtue of bearing the child and the man by virtue of being married to her at the time. Consider what we have here: a woman has claim because she bears the child; a man's claim depends on his being married to the woman; but a woman can realize her claim only if her husband pays the midwife and realizes his claim; otherwise she forfeits her claim to the wife of the man who acquires the fatherhood by paying the midwife. Here is an intricate chain of dependence and contingency, the whole resting ultimately on the idea that a woman has a claim to a child she bears, provided she is eligible to bear it and is otherwise qualified to assert the bearer's claim.

The Mota example emphasizes again that the related phenomena of family and kinship organization, in all their complexity and variety, derive from the association of women and children in the natural sequence of parturition and nursing and from the attachments that develop therefrom, and also from the association of men and women as their sex partners in marriage.

CONCLUSION

What I have had to say should by now have made some things evident regarding problems of description and comparison in cultural anthropology. We start armed with the concepts our own culture has given us. We discover that other people make conceptual distinctions that we don't make and that we make distinctions that they don't make. To describe theirs and compare them with ours we have to find a set of concepts capable of describing their distinctions as well as our own. To do this, we have to analyze the phenomena more finely than we had to before, discovering and sorting out variables of which we were previously unaware.

Linguists encountered the same problem when they began to describe the speech sounds of other languages. For a time they engaged in meaningless arguments as to whether a sound in Hawaiian, for example, was equivalent to English *r* or to English *l,* for they had no other way of talking about what they heard. Eventually, they teased apart the variables that go into sound production, arriving at a kit of phonetic distinctions in terms of which the meaningful categories of sound of any particular language—its so-called phonemes—can be described, and in terms of which those of different languages can be compared, with their differences and similarities precisely delimited.[21]

I have sought to illustrate what is involved in the task of developing a similar kit of analytical concepts for describing and comparing the meaningful distinctions in different cultures that relate to social relationships connected with human reproduction. I have done so with reference to certain hoary problems of definition in anthropology.

The definitions I offer are not presented as the best definitions in any absolute sense. They are the best definitions I have been able to find that simultaneously serve two purposes. One is that they be universally applicable and provide fixed reference points for general comparison. The other purpose is that within the limitations imposed by universal applicability the definitions retain as much as possible of the considerations we have traditionally had in mind when we have identified something in another culture as the analogue of what we call marriage, family, and parenthood in our own culture. For purposes other than these different definitions will be appropriate.

21. As presented, for example, by Bloch and Trager (1942) and Pike (1943).

More important than this, I have tried to reveal some of the finer conceptual distinctions that we have to make for clear descriptions and controlled comparison, regardless of what we chose to refer to by "marriage," "family," and "parenthood." The exercise has shown that the basic concepts for comparison and description of the phenomena in question are of at least two kinds. Rights and duties are one—the things out of which different social entitlements are constructed and to which social transactions pertain. They are among the formal universal elements of culture. Problems with which all human societies have to deal make up the other set of basic concepts. They provide the universal topics for which people find it useful and even necessary to define rights and duties. They are the functional universals—the concerns with respect to which people maintain cultures. In the context of this discussion, they are the things that follow from sexual dimorphism, sexual reproduction, parturition, formation of emotional attachments, processes of physical and social maturation, male dominance, and male competition for sexual access to females.

I have chosen to define marriage, family, and parenthood with reference to particular combinations of these basic analytical concepts with the object, as I have said, of making the fewest departures from the traditional import of these terms and yet giving them general applicability for description and comparison. I do not imply that all concepts must be universally applicable; but some must, for otherwise no general propositions about the nature of man as a social animal are possible. And in the search for general propositions, generations of anthropologists have sought to use the concepts under discussion as if they were universally applicable, even when their definitions failed entirely to make them so.

2. Kindred and Clan

IMPLICIT in the writings of early anthropologists is the idea that a society's rules relating to proprietary rights in children and to membership in groups of kinsmen are a direct reflection of the form of family organization. A society's form of family organization, in turn, is regarded as a direct reflection of its members' conception of parenthood (especially fatherhood); and this conception is assumed to depend on what the society's members understand about the biological facts of procreation. Anthropologists used the term "descent" to refer to theories of biological kinship, forms of family organization, rules of kin group membership, and rules of succession to political office and to social and property entitlements as if they were all necessarily reflections of the same thing. And so they largely were, of course, in Euro-American folk ideology and law. But there is no natural logical reason why they should be so viewed, and many other peoples in the world treat them independently.

Nineteenth-century anthropologists themselves, of course, had what we now perceive to be quite erroneous ideas about the biological facts of procreation and genetic relationship. They knew nothing of modern genetics and took for granted the European folk theory that biological kinship is based on ties of "common blood." We are still trying to free ourselves from the constraints of nineteenth-century thought in this matter. Our technical terminology, for example, continues to use the word "consanguinity" to refer to relationships that involve a connection exclusively through a chain of parent-child ties. Twentieth-century anthropology has been left a legacy of assumptions and associated vocabulary that takes them for granted.

According to these assumptions, descent (not distinguished from biological kinship) was first traced only through women, because people were unaware of physical paternity. In keeping with this, the family was "matriarchal," consisting of a woman and her children, with such responsibilities as men were needed to perform being performed by the woman's brothers. Genealogical kinship was traced only through a chain of mother-child links and thus was "matrilineal." Since organized groups of kinsmen could be related only in this way, they, too, were matrilineal. Succession to office and inheritance of property, insofar as they were based on kinship, were also matrilineal, necessarily following a line of transmission from mother to daughter and from maternal uncle to sister's son. In time, recognition of biological paternity, coupled with technological developments that gave greater economic power to men and promoted the importance of such masculine activities as warfare and government, led to increasing male dominance in the domestic sphere. The result was a "patriarchal" family organization, polygyny, emphasis on the father-child tie in reckoning genealogical kinship or descent, and minimization of the mother-child tie. In some cases, as in parts of Europe, there was even outright denial of a "blood tie" between mother and child. Kin groups were now "parilineal"; and succession to office and inheritance of property were from father to son or, in extreme cases, from father's sister to brother's daughter. Finally, recognition of the equal biological contribution of both father and mother led to the monogamous family, with husband and wife in a more egalitarian relationship. Genealogical kinship or descent was now traced equally through both parents to a circle of relatives on all sides and was hence "bilateral." These three ways of reckoning kinship or descent with their presumed associated institutions were assumed to have a temporal relationship, the bilateral having emerged out of the patrilineal and the patrilineal having emerged out of the matrilineal. Therefore, they represented three major stages in the evolutionary development of human society.[1]

Anthropologists subsequently disputed the idea that they represented distinct evolutionary stages, but they did not dispute the validity of the syndromes themselves. They continued to equate descent with kinship and to link them with rules of membership in kin groups and with rules of succession and inheritance. Whole societies were still classified as matrilineal, patrilineal, or bilateral (e.g., Murdock 1949). We may know better than to do this now, but the manner of speaking is still very much with us. Furthermore, until the last decade, it was still assumed by anthropologists that kin groups had to be either matrilineal, patrilineal, or bilateral. There were no other possibilities. When they went out to do field work, most ethnographers felt that as soon as they had enough information to decide whether a particular group was patrilineal, matrilineal, or bilateral, they had satisfactorily described its membership principles. Relatively few were concerned to find what the membership principles actually were and to describe them apart from the anthropological pigeonhole they were supposed to put the society in.

Rivers (1924:86) and, after him, Murdock (1949:15) have pointed out that descent as a theory of kinship and descent as a principle for allocating membership in a functioning social group are two distinct things and should not be confused. They used the term descent to refer to principles of membership in kin groups. Very recently Fox (1967:52) has again stressed that ideas of kinship and principles of succession and group membership do not necessarily coincide. Observation by ethnographers of societies in which there are both patrilineal and matrilineal kin groups at the same time, moreover, led Murdock (1940) to characterize such societies as having "double descent." This fourth category, he claimed, exhausted the possible ways societies could be classified according to their use of descent principles for membership in kin groups (Murdock 1949:15).

---

1. Morgan (1877) presented the most systematic elaboration of these stages in a widely read and influential book.

Over a decade ago, I observed that membership in kin groups or in other social units and categories based on kinship[2] is in fact more complicated (Goodenough 1955). I argued that there are fundamentally two different kinds of kin group. In one kind all the members have an ancestor in common and are therefore all related to one another through an unbroken chain of parent-child ties—ties of what we may continue to call consanguinity. Such a group can perpetuate itself readily by adding to it the children of existing members. In the other type of group, the members have a kinsman in common but are not necessarily all related to one another; they do not share a common ancestor. Its existence as a group lasts only as long as its members have some common responsibilities to their common kinsman, usually only during the latter's lifetime. It seemed appropriate to me to call the kind of group that is based on a common ancestor a "descent group," since it is comprised of someone's descendants. The kind of group that is based on a common kinsman, however, is clearly not a descent group in this sense. Yet up to that time, it had been presented as the prime example of groups based on bilateral descent (e.g., Murdock 1949). My concern at the time was to show that there are groups based on a common ancestor that are not unilineal—are neither patrilineal nor matrilineal—and at the same time should not be confused with groups based on a common kinsman, as had been the case theretofore. Such groups, I observed, are widely represented in the Pacific Islands.[3] I referred to them as nonunilineal descent groups, avoiding use of the term bilateral, which had already become so firmly attached to groups based on a common kinsman.

By that time, however, there had developed in social anthropology a body of propositions relating to what were called lineages

2. For brevity's sake I shall hereafter use the expression "kin group" to refer to all social divisions and culturally defined aggregations of persons for which ties of kinship are among the criteria of membership. There is no need in this discussion to distinguish "groups" in a narrow sociological sense from other kinds of social division or category, as Scheffler (1966) has argued we must. Their status as corporations, as solidary bodies, as entities whose members all assemble in connection with activities of some kind is, of course, germane for some discussions, but not for this one.

3. Young (1968) has shown that I was wrong about one example I presented of nonunilineal descent groups in the Pacific, namely the Bwaidoga of Goodenough Island, whose descent groups he shows to be patrilineal.

(Radcliffe-Brown 1950, Fortes 1953). These propositions were formulated largely in the study of certain African societies perceived, according to existing anthropological stereotypes, as having patrilineal descent groups or lineages (Evans-Pritchard 1940, Fortes 1945, 1949). And within the limitations of earlier theory, lineages could be only either patrilineal or matrilineal; bilateral descent could not produce lineages at all.[4] Social anthropologists had thus acquired an investment in a particular conception of ancestor-based groups as essentially unilineal, succinctly stated by Radcliffe-Brown (1950:82) as follows:

> Cognatic [bilateral] systems are rare, not only in Africa but in the world at large. The reasons have already been indicated: it is difficult to establish and maintain a wide-range system on a purely cognatic basis; it is only a unilateral system that will permit the division of a society into separate organized kin-groups.

This being the climate of thinking into which the idea of non-unilineal descent groups was introduced, an extended discussion ensued.

On the one hand, examples of nonunilineal groups or of descent groups that did not meet classical unilineal criteria began to be reported in profusion (Firth 1957, 1963; Ember 1959; Solien 1959; Glasse 1959; Murdock, ed., 1960; Chowning 1962; Scheffler 1962, 1965; Groves 1963a; Langness 1964; Lambert 1966; Lloyd 1966; Keesing 1968), and questions were raised about the adequacy of lineage theory (Barnes 1962, Brown 1962, de Lepervanche 1967–68).

At the same time, confusion was added. "Cognatic descent" was suggested as an appropriate designation of the membership principles in nonunilineal descent groups (Murdock 1960:2), as if they were all alike in their principles of reckoning descent. Radcliffe-Brown (1950) had already used "cognatic descent" as a synonym for "bilateral descent" in connection with groups based on a

4. The patrilineal emphasis of this work led to an examination of societies with matrilineal lineages, whose results were published by Schneider and Gough (1961) in a large work entitled *Matrilineal Kinship*. Even so recently, the equation of kinship with descent is made in the title of a major anthropological work!

common kinsman, which, following the Anglo-Saxon example, he saw as formed by the several "stocks" (a stock being the descendants of a common ancestor) to which an individual belongs by virtue of his multiple ancestry. "Cognatic descent" continued to be used as a synonym for "bilateral descent"; and groups based on a common kinsman tended to be lumped together again with nonunilineal descent groups in the traditional bilateral bin of nineteenth-century anthropology (e.g., Bohannan 1963:127). Now there were unilineal descent groups, which were properly called "lineages," in which membership was ascribed and to which lineage theory obtained; and over against them there were cognatic descent groups, which included an odd assortment of ancestor-based groups, referred to as "ambilineal ramages" (following a suggestion by Firth 1957), in which membership was presumed to be optional, and also groups based on a common kinsman, now referred to as "personal kindreds" (following the usage of Leach 1950).

This lumping together of nonunilineal groups and personal kindreds as all representing cognatic descent was especially confusing in view of the argument against the idea of nonunilineal descent groups put forth by defenders of classical lineage theory. For groups to be properly called descent groups, they said, membership must be automatic and not a matter of choice, by which they seem to have meant that membership must be a fact of kinship, equating descent and kinship (Fortes 1959). Indeed, descent was defined as "automatic recruitment by virtue of status at birth" (Leach 1962:131). This put them back into the nineteenth-century position that descent (kinship) can be reckoned through males only, through females only, or through males and females equally—that is descent may be patrilineal, matrilineal, or cognatic (bilateral).

With this in mind, Freeman (1961:200) argued that unless the membership of nonunilineal descent groups is equally through males and females, as in the case of a cognatic stock, it is "an error of analysis" to consider them as "defined by cognatic descent." He continued that "unless some criterion other than, and in addition to, descent be brought into operation, it is impossible to achieve the division of society into discrete groupings" with nonunilineal descent groups. Thus he implied that with unilineal descent groups there is no other criterion of membership in addition to descent itself (which is patrilineal, matrilineal, or cognatic). He further implied that for groups to qualify as descent groups they must be without overlap of membership. Since this is impossible for cognatic stocks, unless they are endogamous, unilineal descent provides the only basis for effectively functioning *descent* groups, as Radcliffe-Brown, quoted above, said. Most reported instances of nonunilineal descent groups, therefore, cannot properly be called descent groups because they are not based on descent, about which there can be no options, but on choices relating to entitlements based on "filiation" (Fortes 1959, Goody 1961, Peranio 1961, Leach 1962).

Filiation got into the picture because of the old confusion of descent and kinship. Describing kinship among the Tallensi, Fortes (1949) distinguished ties to fellow clansmen (based on patrilineal descent) from functionally different and complementary ties to relatives through one's mother. With this distinction in mind, he later (1953) proposed the term "complementary filiation" as a principle other than descent by which kinsmen were recognized as kinsmen. Filiation is the fact of being one's parent's child. Fortes added (1953:33) that "we all now take it for granted that filiation— by contrast with descent—is universally bilateral," because everyone has two parents. In this he seemed to equate descent with membership in unilineal lineages and clans and to equate filiation with Radcliffe-Brown's cognatic kinship. Later discussion has tended to follow more closely Freeman's (1958:fn. 9) definition of filiation as "the system whereby an individual establishes membership of a structurally continuing group by virtue of birth (or adoption) and with reference to one of his (or her) parents" (compare with Leach's definition of descent, cited above). The difference between descent and filiation, thus defined, was no longer a matter of unilineal as against bilateral connection but a matter of status or entitlement by virtue of ancestry (descent) as distinct from entitlement by virtue of parentage (filiation).[5]

---

5. See the excellent review by Davenport (1963). I must add that as Freeman defined it, filiation is not really in opposition to descent but is rather the parental connection through which a person becomes a member of a group or acquires any other jural or social entitlement, including his socially recognized kinship with other persons. If the "structurally continuing group" of

Membership in nonunilineal descent groups, then, was to be understood as a matter of entitlement through parentage and not a matter of status by virtue of ancestry. By this reasoning, lineage theory was presumably saved, and nonunilineal descent groups could be dismissed as not being descent groups, properly speaking, at all.

These arguments have been satisfactorily answered in large part by Firth (1963), Forde (1963), Scheffler (1964, 1966), Schneider (1965), and Fox (1967), and by the growing body of empirical evidence. But some misconceptions remain; and in their review of the matter, Buchler and Selby (1968:91–98) have pointed to a need to set aside past terms and concepts and to analyze the variables whose different combinations produce the wide variety of organizational forms we actually find. There is reason therefore for me to come back to the matter I broached in 1955 and to consider some things I see as highly relevant to the description and comparison of kin groups but that continue to be confused or neglected by many anthropologists.

First of all, I must insist that my division of kin groups into those based on a common ancestor (descent groups) and those based on a common kinsman (kindreds) is a fundamental one of great theoretical utility. The division into unilineal and cognatic groups on the other hand is neither fundamental nor theoretically helpful. Membership in descent groups, whether they are unilineal or nonunilineal, involves principles relating to the inclusion and exclusion of descendants of the focal ancestor; membership in

---

which a person becomes a member through filiation was founded by unrelated persons, then its subsequent members by filiation are not all related to one another, nor are they descended from a common ancestor, and the group is not a descent group. If, in time, the members come to think of themselves as having had a common ancestor and as, therefore, being all related to one another, the group becomes a descent group thereby. If the group was actually founded by one person, the membership by filiation guarantees that the members will be descended from him, and the group is necessarily a descent group. All descent groups, unilineal and nonunilineal, involve filiation as the basis of membership; but filiation may also be the basis of membership in other than descent groups, as in some trade unions. From this point of view there is reason to reconsider the status of dispersed patrilineal and matrilineal clans, phratries, and moieties—at least in some societies—as descent groups or descent categories. Speaking of the "matri-

kindreds involves principles relating to the inclusion and exclusion of persons connected by genealogical (including marital) ties to the focal kinsman. These principles are necessarily different, at least in part, for the two kinds of group. The greater the generation depth of a descent group, the greater is the genealogical distance between its living members. Genealogical distance cannot, therefore, be a consideration in the inclusion and exclusion of descendants.[6] Genealogical distance, however, is the most common criterion by which people account themselves in or out of someone's kindred.

I have little to add to what Davenport (1959, 1964:83–85), Mitchell (1963), Keesing (1966), and Fox (1967) have already said about kindreds. Therefore, I shall discuss them briefly, now, and then direct most of my attention to descent groups.

KINDREDS

In traditional anthropological thinking, kindreds have been seen as based on a reckoning of kinship equally in all genealogical directions through both male and female links. The results of such reckoning is a circle of relatives around some focal person. Who is included in the circle and who excluded is determined by a principle of genealogical distance. My third cousins might be included in my kindred, for example, but my fourth cousins fall outside it. With this in mind and assuming that genealogical distance is always uniformly applied as a criterion, Freeman (1961) has followed Radcliffe-

---

lineal sibs" (clans) of the Lakalai, Chowning (1966:477–478) has said, "the Lakalai sibs have no tradition of descent from a single common ancestor. The people are generally uninterested in origins, and even in myths it is assumed that the present system always existed, with each sib containing numerous members. There are various accounts of life in the *olu* [associated topographical feature to which the spirits of sib members return after death], and occasionally it may be stated that a sib originated at or from its *olu*. When questioned, informants said that presumably sibmates must have shared a remote ancestress, but they knew nothing about her. However, the 'traditional bond of common descent' (Murdock 1949:47) is acknowledged, and presumably derivation from a single person is not essential to the definition of the sib." In this case it is hard to say whether we are dealing with matrilineal or with what should be called matrifilial divisions of society.

6. Genealogical distance may play a role in the formal definition of lineage segments in a segmentary lineage system such as Evans-Pritchard (1940) has described for the Nuer of Africa.

Brown (1950) in looking on kindreds as resulting from the overlap of a set of "cognatic stocks," each stock being the set of someone's descendants. Thus a kindred that included second cousins but excluded third cousins would consist of the descendants of all of the focal kinsman's great-grandparents, the descendants of any one married pair of great-grandparents constituting a stock. Freeman thus specifically excluded relatives by marriage. But kindreds so defined—by generalization from the Anglo-Saxon mode of reckoning —are empirically only a special case of kin groups and/or kin categories based on having a relative in common. Relatives by marriage are included in one's kindred in Truk; and the degrees of genealogical distance that bound a kindred need not be the same on the father's side and on the mother's side.

Fox (1967), Keesing (1966), and I (1961a) have all called attention to kindreds restricted by the use of membership criteria in addition to the criterion of genealogical distance. The Kalmuk Mongols represent an extreme case, having kindreds in which only relatives through males are included, extending out so many degrees of genealogical distance (Aberle 1953, Adelman 1954). Thus they add a principle of unisexual linkage to a principle of genealogical distance. Freedman's account (1958:41) of the "agnatic *wu fu*" of southeastern China provides a clear example of such a kindred, also; and the "truncated patrilineages" or *kitaata* of the Congolese Suku (Kopytoff 1964:107) can also be regarded as small kindreds bounded by considerations of generational distance and unisexual linkage in addition to genealogical distance.

Distance from the focal kinsman, moreover, can be reckoned by means other than simply counting the number of genealogical links. A Lakalai of New Britain (Goodenough 1962, Chowning and Goodenough 1966) includes within his kindred all members of his hamlet—regardless of how tenuous the actual kinship ties—as well as those of his genealogically near kin who happen to live in other hamlets. A person of Romónum, Truk, in Micronesia includes in his kindred his grandparents, his grandchildren, and all the members of his matrilineal lineage and of his father's matrilineal lineage (Goodenough 1951:102–103). He also includes the children and grandchildren of men of his own and his father's matrilineal lineages. Here the boundaries of descent groups are used to determine genealogical distance as a principle of kindred membership.

The Lakalai of New Britain illustrate something about kindreds that has often been overlooked. Each Lakalai has an immediate kindred, whose members have a number of important obligations to him and he to them. He also has a more extended kindred, whose members have fewer obligations to him.[7] Beyond this is an even more extended circle of people to whom he relates socially in terms of one or another type of kin relationships. Indeed, all peaceful social relationships are conducted within the idiom of kinship, so that an adult Lakalai can classify anyone with whom he has continuing social dealings as some kind of kinsman, including everyone in his community. A man almost inevitably marries someone whom he already counts as a nominal kinswoman. Such, also, is the case for Moala in Fiji (Sahlins 1962), for Australian aboriginal tribes (Radcliffe-Brown 1930–31), for the endogamous and commensal local castes of Ceylon (Yalman 1962, 1967), and for the /Kung Bushmen of southern Africa (L. Marshall 1959). This open-ended extension of kin relationships makes it possible to develop extended kindreds in which membership is effectively bounded not by genealogical distance but by practical geographical and social constraints on social intercourse.

This kind of arrangement can be viewed from quite different perspectives. Subjectively, from the individual's viewpoint, there is an extended circle of nominal kinsmen in his social field of operations; objectively, from a social viewpoint, relationships within local and territorial groups are organized on the model of kin relationships. Thus local groups can be organized as groups of kinsmen, and often are. Kindreds as well as descent groups may provide the models for such organization. We anthropologists have habitually looked at such groups primarily as kin groups and only secondarily as local groups. We have talked about "localized kin groups" but rarely about kin-structured local groups (Goodenough 1962, Helm 1965).[8] Coming at these phenomena from more than

7. Similar circles of kindred are reported for the Kwaio of the Solomon Islands by Keesing (1966). These circles may be compared with the differing degrees of "sibship" described by Radcliffe-Brown (1950:16) for Anglo-Saxon kindreds.

8. I should point out that in citing my account (1962) of Lakalai hamlet organization as an example of a local group organized by kinship principles, Buchler and Selby (1968:88) have given the expression "nodal kindred" a different meaning from the one I had in mind when I used it to characterize

one vantage point should enhance the quality of our work in both description and comparison.

I have always assumed, along with my fellow anthropologists, that an individual must be the focal referent of a kindred. But Keesing's (1970a) account of the Kwaio suggests that descent groups can be the focal referent of kindred-like units as well. A Kwaio descent group or lineage consists of all those lineal descendants of a founding ancestor who have "primary rights" in a tract of land or territory. Ideally, they are patrilineally descended from the founding ancestor, but in practice they often include persons descended through female links. In addition to a lineage's members there are living descendants of past members (usually but not always female past members) who do not have "primary rights" and who are not members of the lineage, but they have "secondary rights," including use rights, in the lineage's estate. The number of parent-child links between them and the ancestor who was last a member affects the strength of their "secondary rights," and after several generations' remove, the secondary rights lapse. Thus around each lineage, there is a circle of nonmember kinsmen that is limited by considerations of genealogical distance. Kinsmen in this circle have claims by virtue of kinship on the estate of the lineage. Thus each Kwaio lineage may be seen as having its lineage-based kindred, just as each Kwaio individual has his personal kindred (Keesing 1966).

The situation among the Kwaio is exactly like that where title to an estate passes down a line of individuals, while the personal kin-

---

a hamlet. According to them, "Each hamlet takes its 'character' from the set of siblings that make up its core, and sibs that do not have enough men to warrant their forming a sibling set will relate themselves to the core. For this reason the organization is called *nodal*." What they say of the hamlet is not untrue, but it is not the reason I called the organization "nodal." Each Lakalai's personal kindred includes the descendants (with their spouses) of the men and women who were in the same siblings sets with his grandparents. It also includes all of his hamlet mates, regardless of how distantly they are related to him genealogically. The residents of a hamlet are thus all members of every resident's kindred and are all kindred mates to one another. In this way the local group or hamlet is the part of every resident's kindred that overlaps with every other resident's kindred. This large area of overlap is the "node" to which I had reference when I called the Lakalai hamlet a "nodal kindred."

dred of each successive title holder has use rights or other secondary rights in the estate. Such a temporal succession of overlapping kindreds of successive title holders has the semblance of a continuing body with an interest in an estate. Davenport (1959: 565) has proposed the term "stem kindred" for this kind of continuing body. The Kwaio example shows that the title holder at the core of a stem kindred can be a corporation, in this case a lineage, as well as an individual.

DESCENT GROUPS

I wish now to turn to descent groups. By a descent group I mean any publicly recognized social entity such that being a lineal descendant of a particular real or fictive ancestor is a criterion of membership.[9] By a descendant, I mean someone who traces a connection to someone as ancestor through a series of jurally relevant parent-child links, whatever may be the rules for establishing the relevance of those links in particular societies.

A descent group that is "pure" in the sense that descent is the sole criterion of membership must consist of all the descendants of the focal ancestor, whether they are descended through men or women. A pure descent group is thus similar in form to what I have referred to already as a "stock" (Radcliffe-Brown 1950:16, 22; Freeman 1961; Fox 1967:168–169), the difference being that it is not simply a device for determining kindred boundaries but a recognized group or social category contrasting with other groups or categories and has specific functions of some kind.

In an endogamous community, the course of time will produce an increasing overlap of membership in such groups, until eventually everyone is descended from all the founding ancestors and the several descent groups have become congruent in membership and coterminous with the community itself. If there was a famous leader among the founding ancestors, everyone may claim to be of his stock, the several ancestors being merged into one. The relatively

9. All descent groups are in this respect "lineal," whether they are unilineal or nonunilineal, as Firth (1963:26) has observed. Maybury-Lewis (1960:191) has referred to "cognatic descent" as "alineal descent," but he evidently had kindreds rather than nonunilineal descent groups in mind.

endogamous territorial groups or local "tribes" of some Polynesian islands, including the *hapu* of the New Zealand Maori as described by Firth (1963), may well have arisen in this way. Since such groups are not entirely endogamous, there are bound to be some individuals who can claim membership in more than one. But within any one, the particular genealogical path by which he reckons back to the founding ancestor can make no difference in his group membership, although it may make a difference in his social rank within the group. Approximating this arrangement, also, are some of the valley communities of the Kentucky mountains (Kutsche 1960), in which all persons accounted as members, as distinct from outsiders, must have one parent who was accounted a member, and so on back to the original settlers from whom all members are by now equally descended. This preserves in Kentucky what seems to have been characteristic of at least some English village communities in the middle ages. Homans (1941:122–123) cites an instance in which an outsider had acquired a tenement in a village. When he died, his brother, also not of the "blood of the village," was his next of kin and heir, but the village members argued that according to local custom the deceased's sister's son should take precedence, for the former holder's sister had married a man who was of the blood of the village, and in cases where the nearer kinsman was not of the blood of the village the tenement should go to a more distant one who was.

Such relatively unrestricted and territorially associated descent groups correspond with what Murdock (1949:62–64) has called "demes," although he arrived at them conceptually in a way that did not differentiate them from the extended kindreds to which I alluded above.[10]

But social groups exist because people have jobs for them to do. For some purposes overlapping membership poses no problems, but for other purposes it is better for groups not to overlap. Standing work groups active in daily domestic economic activities must be mutually exclusive in membership. So must any political or military group that demands the undivided loyalties of its members. But property-holding groups can readily overlap, just as someone

10. I have discussed this in my review (1961a:1346) of *Social Structure in Southeast Asia,* edited by Murdock.

in our society can easily be a shareholder and member of the board of several corporations at once. Overlapping or not, however, if descent groups eventually become coterminous with the community, the community in effect takes over their functions and they cease to exist as separate social entities. Such is quite possible when the functions are religious, for example. But if their functions demand that descent groups remain significantly smaller in membership than the community as a whole, then some principles for restricting membership are needed.

Whatever the restricting principle is, it is not the idea of descent. That I should have to say such an obvious thing will strike many as strange. I say it for the benefit of my fellow anthropologists. For we are such captives of our own jargon that, as I indicated earlier, some of us seem to believe that the principles of patrilineality and matrilineality include no other considerations than descent itself (e.g., Freeman 1961, Leach 1962, Goody 1968). We have talked about these principles as rules of descent for so long that we appear to have lost sight of what we are really talking about, namely application of the criterion of sex as a means of restricting membership to only some of a focal ancestor's descendants.[11] Fox (1967:49) has aptly observed that unilineal linkage is "unisexual linkage," and that this characterization "is perhaps less confusing as a general description."

Indeed, the traditional division into patrilineal, matrilineal, and bilateral or cognatic principles of descent has served to confuse the idea of being descended from an ancestor with the use (or nonuse) of sex as jurally relevant for reckoning one's lineage to an ancestor. Consequently we have been unable to consider that sex may be only one among a number of different considerations jurally relevant for tracing one's ancestry. Buchler and Selby (1968:90) have said, "Unilineal groups stress one-sex ties . . . whereas nonunilineal groups make use of either." Thus they miss the point that sex ties

11. Leach, himself, has called attention to this problem, observing (1961:3): "Ever since Morgan began writing of the Iroquois, it has been customary for anthropologists to distinguish unilineal from nonunilineal descent systems, and among the former to distinguish patrilineal societies from matrilineal societies. These categories now seem to us so rudimentary and obvious that it is extremely difficult to break out of the straitjacket of thought which the categories themselves impose."

may be entirely irrelevant in nonunilineal groups. On the other hand, Scheffler (1966:544), while usefully distinguishing what he calls "descent-constructs" from "descent-phrased rules" and "descent-ordered units," has written, "Cognatic descent-constructs are those in which sex of the linking kinsman at each step is immaterial for the tracing of the continuum and the continuum itself is significant." Thus he explicitly made a type out of the irrelevance of sex without regard to what else, besides sex, may be relevant.

I do not mean to imply that sex is unimportant. The great frequency with which people use sex as a criterion for restricting the membership of descent groups is undoubtedly largely responsible for the confusion to which I have just alluded. As a legitimate type, moreover, unilineal descent groups are theoretically interesting, and they may, on occasion, be meaningfully contrasted with all other types. But this fact does not permit us to make a basic type of all the remaining types. Therefore, I shall continue to speak of nonunilineal descent groups, rather than of cognatic or ambilineal ones, in order to emphasize that we are not dealing with a specific type of reckoning but with a residual category that contains at least several different modes of reckoning.

As for sex as a criterion for restricting membership in descent groups, it can be used in several different ways. An obvious way is to restrict membership in a descent group in each succeeding generation to the children of those members who are of a particular sex: to the children of the men but not to the children of the women, or to the children of the women but not to the children of the men. If new membership is restricted to the children of female members, all members of the group are linked to one another through women and the group is a matrilineal descent group. If new membership is restricted to the children of male members, all members are linked to one another through men and the group is a patrilineal descent group. It is also possible to include only the male children of male members and only the female children of female members, a pattern that has been called "parallel descent." It has been reported for the Apinayé of Brazil (Nimuendajú 1939, Maybury-Lewis 1960).[12] Still another possibility is to include only the female children of male members and only the male children of female members.

12. But see the comments by Fox (1967:143–145).

Something similar to this has been reported for the Mundugamor of
New Guinea (Mead 1935) in connection with the inheritance of
property other than land, but there is question as to whether we are
dealing with descent groups here or with rules governing the inheritance of property (Fox 1967:139–140).

These ways of using sex to restrict membership in descent groups
create important differences in how immediate kin are brought together in the same groups. With the patrilineal and matrilineal
modes of restriction, one sex shares the same descent-group membership with all its children, while the other sex shares it with none.
In the cases exemplified by the Apinayé and Mundugamor, each
sex gets to share descent-group membership with some of its children. The latter effect is also accomplished by another device
reported by Kennedy (1937:291) for the Buginese and Macassar
area of Celebes. Here, membership in what are presumably descent
groups is restricted to the odd-numbered children of female members and to the even-numbered children of male members.
Obviously, in patrilineal and matrilineal cases, siblings are always
kept together as members of the same descent group; but in the
other cases, siblings are divided either by sex or by birth-order.
This, as Fox (1967:140–143) implies in his thoughtful discussion,
may account for the extreme rarity of the latter means of using sex
as a restricting criterion.[13]

With unilineal descent groups, then, membership is restricted
simply by a criterion of parental sex. With descent groups of
Apinayé or Mundugamor type, membership is restricted by a combination of two criteria: parental sex and filial sex. And with the
Buginese, membership is restricted by parental sex in combination
with a criterion of oddness/evenness of filial birth-order.[14]

As I have said, there are criteria other than sex by which children
of a descent group's members may be included or excluded as new
members. On the atoll of Onotoa in the southern Gilbert Islands,
for example, it is my understanding that in precolonial times if a

13. From this point of view, the rarity of other than the unilineal mode of
using sex to restrict descent-group membership is in keeping with Radcliffe-
Brown's (1930–31:44; 1941) idea that sibling solidarity and the social
equivalence of siblings are basic considerations in social organization.
14. Murdock (1949:45) cites the Apinayé, Mundugamor, and Buginese as
examples of differing combinations of patrilineal and matrilineal principles.

man continued to reside after marriage on the ancestral estate associated with his descent group, called a *kaainga,* his children belonged to his *kaainga.* But if he moved in marriage to the ancestral estate associated with his wife's *kaainga,* his children belonged to it rather than to his own. In other words, the children of *kaainga* members who remained on the *kaainga* lands after they married were added as members, while the children of members who moved away from their *kaainga* lands to those of their spouses were excluded as members.

The *kaainga* of Onotoa were obviously not unilineal, for the connecting genealogical links between two members or between a member and the focal ancestor were not necessarily all of one sex. Sex was not the directly relevant factor. The rule of succession to leadership in the *kaainga,* however, was that it could go only through males. Therefore, between the head man of a *kaainga* and its focal ancestor there were only male links. Some anthropologists would describe these groups, therefore, as mixed, having a so-called agnatic core but allowing for "cognatic" recruitment of members as well. This confuses principles of membership with principles of succession to office. But the preponderance of membership through fathers in Onotoan *kaainga* goes beyond the senior line. In the inheritance of land rights, the bulk of the combined parental holdings is divided among the sons, with the eldest getting more than the younger sons. If there is enough land, each daughter may receive a plot as dowry; otherwise only the oldest daughter receives one. Daughters come into sizable inheritances in land only in the absence of sons. The rules of inheritance, therefore, strongly favor residence on the estate associated with the husband's *kaainga,* because that is where the bulk of the married couple's holdings are likely to be concentrated, especially if the husbands are first-born sons whose fathers were first-born sons. The preponderantly agnatic core of the Onotoan *kaainga,* therefore, seems to have been a consequence of rules of succession to office and of rules of inheritance in land as these affected decisions regarding marital residence. The agnatic (patrilineal) core is thus in itself irrelevant for classifying the group according to its membership rules, as Scheffler (1966) has also observed.

This calls attention to a major problem plaguing comparative study in cultural anthropology: failure to specify exactly what the purpose of the comparison is and what are the considerations for classifying things (in this case descent groups) that are relevant to that purpose. If I am concerned with the possible influence on kinship terminology of the prevalence of male links between a group's members, then I shall treat the Onotoan *kaainga* as essentially like a patrilineal lineage; for the incidence of female links between members of a *kaainga* is low and there are no such links in the senior line within it. My concern in this case would not be with cultural principles of membership but with the frequency of male and female links between members that result from the operation of these principles in practice. I would be concerned with statistical similarities among the social outputs of cultures. Different cultural (including jural) principles can produce statistically similar outputs; and the same cultural principles can produce statistically different outputs in different circumstances. When we set about comparing communities, societies, or ethnic groups, therefore, it is essential that we be clear as to whether our problem calls for comparison of social outputs or of cultural principles. Some investigations call for one and some for the other. Unfortunately, a good deal of the argument about descent groups has failed to take account of this. (I shall come back to this matter in a more general context in my last chapter.)

The descent groups just described for Onotoa in the Gilbert Islands resemble unilineal lineages in that they do not overlap their membership. An individual, moreover, has no options about his membership. His parents had an option as to their post-marital residence, and his membership follows from their choice; but he has no choice himself, as far as I know.[15] Choice relates to residence, not to *kaainga* membership.

I mention this, because some social anthropologists have claimed that nonunilineal descent groups necessarily involve choice and that this makes them structurally different from unilineal descent groups. In his otherwise excellent account of nonunilineal (his cognatic) descent groups, Fox (1967:147–163) makes just such an assertion.

---

15. If I am in error about the Onotoan case, the point remains that membership based on a principle of parental choice of residence (or anything else) need not involve any choice by an individual regarding his own descent-group membership. A detailed account of the *kaainga* in the northern Gilbert Islands has been provided by Lambert (1966).

He goes on to show how discrete nonunilineal lineages can result from certain modes of restriction; but he does not admit the possibility that an individual may be without choice regarding his membership.

Actually, the presence and absence of choice depend on quite different considerations and are not a function of the distinction between unilineal and nonunilineal descent.

THE ROLE OF RIGHTS AND DUTIES

Absence of choice may be because membership is not a consequence of a jural consideration at all, in that membership is neither the individual's right nor his duty. It may be regarded as a fact of nature, like his sex or skin color, for example. He is what he is, and neither he nor anyone else can change it. Being what he is may have important jural entailments, yet not itself be a product of any jural rule or act; although one can argue that in such cases a person has the duty to his fellow men or to the gods to be what he is. Kinship by "blood" is considered such a fact of nature in Euro-American tradition.[16] The Lakalai of New Britain look similarly on membership in matrilineal clans. There are societies, on the other hand, where membership in descent groups is a consequence of a system of jural obligations. Here the presence and absence of choice depend on whether membership is the individual's right or his duty.

If an individual has a right by virtue of his ancestry to activate membership in more than one descent group, then the

16. Schneider (1968a:27–29)' shows that Americans, for example, make a clear distinction between kinship deriving from "the order of nature" (blood kinship) and kinship deriving from "the order of law" (kinship by marriage). He points out that the people of Yap (1968c), by contrast, regard kinship through females as deriving from their cultural equivalent of our "order of nature," whereas they regard kinship through males as deriving from what we might call an order of nurture. In both societies all of these types of kinship are also a part of the "order of law" to the extent that jural entitlements and rules of conduct are vested in them. What makes a relationship jural is not the mythology about its relation to nature, social contract. spirits, or anything else, but the fact that it involves rights and duties. I think that one of the difficulties in the great debate about descent as against filiation and the relationship of the two to nonunilineal groups has been an unspoken and ethnocentric equation of "descent" with Schneider's "order of nature" and filiation with his "order of law."

chain of connections between pairs of members in any one group cannot in all cases be composed of persons of only one sex. The groups are almost certain to be nonunilineal. In other respects, however, such groups can differ radically in the principles governing eligibility to membership. It is also possible for a person to have the right of membership in only one descent group and still have an option in exercising that right. In a society where this is the way membership works, not everyone need be a member of a descent group.[17] There are societies, too, where only some individuals have the right to belong to descent groups. Firth (1957:4) has observed that in Tonga "by no means every member of the society is a member of a 'lineage'." There are functioning descent groups in the United States—the Du Pont "family" seems to be an example—but few people are eligible to belong to one.

Individual choice disappears when a person has a duty to be a member of a group or, to say it the other way around, when a group has the right to claim him as a member. When a person finds himself a member of a group by ascription, as I have already suggested, the right may be said to lie with his community as a whole, and his is the corresponding duty to comply with the community's rules. Such is ordinarily the case with unilineal descent groups. Such, too, can be the case, as we have seen, with nonunilineal descent groups. But if membership is the individual's right rather than his duty, then individuals have options and the resulting groups are nonunilineal.[18]

When there are options and membership is an individual's right, groups may or may not be overlapping in membership. Onotoa in the Gilbert Islands illustrates both possibilities. In addition to the *kaainga,* which I have just described, there are two other kinds of descent group there. One, called a *bwoti* (usually written *boti*), is a sitting group in the community meeting house. A person's right to membership in a *bwoti* depends on his having inherited a share in a plot of land that carries that right for its shareholders. All shareholders are descended from the original holder, for property rights

17. This seems to be the only circumstance in which unilineal descent groups can result when membership is an individual's right rather than his duty.

18. Firth (1963) has similarly distinguished between "definitive systems" of descent, in which the individual has no choice of membership, and "optative systems," in which the individual has choice.

pass from parent to child, a person getting some from his father (usually the bulk of them) and some from his mother.[19] A person may inherit properties that give him the right to sit in more than one place. He is thus eligible to claim membership in more than one *bwoti*. But he can activate only one such claim at a time. He cannot operate as an active member of two *bwoti* at once. These nonunilineal descent groups, therefore, do not overlap their active memberships.

The remaining kind of nonunilineal descent group in Onotoa is not a corporate body. It consists of all descendants of the original owner of an estate who have kept active their status as descendants. If any present holder of a share of the original estate dies without children, these other descendants can claim it, in order of their genealogical proximity to the deceased former holder. And no member of the group can alienate his share in the ancestral estate without the consent of the other members of the group. The members of such a group all have certain obligations to one another as kinsmen, as members of one another's personal kindreds. As long as a person performs these obligations to the others, he maintains his status as a fellow descendant in good standing; but if he neglects these duties for a significant period of time, he is liable to forfeit his membership rights. Everyone belongs to a number of such groups at once, some with many generations and others with only a few to the focal ancestor. A person keeps up his membership in those from which he and his heirs stand a real chance to gain something, but he does not bother to maintain his standing in those in which he has no prospects.[20]

19. In practice most land rights are passed to sons, daughters receiving only a plot or nothing at all, unless there are no sons, in which case the daughters inherit all their parents' holdings. Consequently, rights to sitting-group membership are acquired more often through one's father than through one's mother. Wives, moreover, have the option of sitting with their husbands, and they usually do. However, I know of a case in which a man changed his active sitting-group membership, for he had the right of membership in more than one; and I know of two full brothers who were active members of two different sitting groups. For a detailed account of the history and organization of Gilbertese meeting houses and a different view of the principles governing membership in their sitting groups, see Maude (1963).

20. These groups also constitute the stocks from which an Onotoan forms his personal kindred. It was my impression in 1951 that such a stock was called an *ooi* (primary meaning "source"), which I later erroneously

Considering membership in descent groups as an individual's right, on the one hand, or an individual's duty, on the other, helps bring into focus some problems relating to memberships in the so-called lineages of some African societies. There are African societies in which a husband acquires proprietary rights in his children, and his children are accounted members of his lineage if he makes the full or big-marriage payment to his wife's relatives; but if he does not give the full payment, his wife's father or brother has proprietary rights in the children, who remain members of their mother's lineage. Because men in these societies regard it as desirable to acquire the proprietary rights in their children and look upon marriage with the full brideprice as the preferred form of marriage, anthropologists have tended to see their lineages as ideally patrilineal and have referred to them as based on a principle of patrilineal descent. From the point of view I have been presenting here, however, membership in these lineages may not follow from a patrilineal principle at all. It may follow, rather, from a rule that people belong to the lineage of the person who has the proprietary rights to their labor, fertility, and loyalty, whoever he may be.

The Okrika Ijo illustrate this well. Their "houses," we saw, recruited as new members the children of women in whose fertility the male members had proprietary rights. A person might belong to the same house as his father or to the same house as his maternal uncle. He might also belong to the same house as his mother's former husband. If he was a slave, he belonged to the same house as his owner; for the rights of a slave owner included proprietary rights to the slave's labor, fertility, and loyalty. Since membership was owed as a duty to the holder of these rights, and since only one person could hold them, membership in the Okrika Ijo houses did not overlap. Furthermore, each house was conceived as an ongoing corporation derived from a founding ancestor, but the chain of "descent" was through a succession of owners of proprietary rights, whether these rights were acquired by sponsoring a

---

published as *oo* (Goodenough 1955), confusing it with the word for "fence"; but I was apparently mistaken in this, Gilbertese using the term *utuu* to refer both to this kind of nonunilineal descent group and to the personal kindred (Lambert 1966:646). I apparently misinterpreted "people of one source" as "people of one group."

girl's puberty ceremony, by inheritance, by purchase in a big-payment marriage, or by the acquisition of a slave. A person's membership in an Ijo house followed from a system of property rights and depended in any given case on the transactions to which these rights had been subjected.

In referring to these houses, Williamson (1962) avoids calling them lineages or descent groups. My point is that in many other African societies, I suspect, anthropologists have interpreted as lineages what can also be seen as groups in which membership is based on property rights in the labor, loyalty, and procreational potential of persons. In an important paper, for example, Jeffreys (1951) noted that in Bantu Africa the institution of *lobolo* has been misnamed "brideprice" (but see Gray 1960). He observes that it stands in contrast to marriage, rather than being a necessary part of it, and is the means whereby a man acquires proprietary rights in his children from his wife's kinsmen. He suggests that *lobolo* is more aptly termed a "child-price." That marriage payments have this function, among others, in many of the so-called patrilineally organized societies of Africa is now generally recognized (e.g., by Fortes 1962), but its implications for descent systems have not been critically evaluated.

In another important paper, Gray (1960) points out that among the Sonjo of eastern Africa, brideprice gives the husband proprietary rights in the wife and her children together. He adds (p. 43),

> According to Sonjo law, children must always stay with their mother; they go with her when she is sold and are adopted by her new husband. Children are priced at four goats apiece, which must be paid to their father by the new husband. These children break most of their agnatic kinship bonds. After the exchange they are not barred from marriage with people of their father's clan, but only with his close relatives. The father himself loses all his rights in his children by a former wife and has no further obligations toward them. The second husband has full authority over his stepchildren. Property inheritance in these cases is through the stepfather. The children are assimilated to his clan and automatically acquire the same kinship bonds with his blood relatives as his other children have. Their relationships with their mother's family remain unchanged.

Among the Sonjo, then, clan membership is governed by owner-ship of the proprietary rights in a woman and her children. As Gray makes clear, these rights may be exchanged or sold in trans-actions involving men of different clan affiliations.

The Okrika Ijo and Sonjo ways of handling group membership are very different from the one I encountered among the Lakalai of New Britain. There, as I have already remarked, membership in matrilineal clans is not affected by or a consequence of jural trans-actions. The clans are believed to have existed from the beginning of time. A person's clan membership cannot be changed, because it is a part of the way the world is ordered. Fellow clansmen owe one another help and hospitality, because they are the same kind of people. Beyond this, however, rights to a person's labor and loyalty are otherwise vested in fatherhood and elder siblinghood in a sys-tem of personal patronage. These rights are largely independent of membership in matrilineal clans, but they affect residence choices and the composition of local groups. The size of a marriage pay-ment does not affect the father's proprietary rights in the child. Similarly in Truk, a child's membership in his mother's lineage cannot be altered by any human transaction. The rights of father-hood and motherhood can be transferred in adoption, and a child can be an operating member of his adoptive mother's lineage, but he does not lose his rights in his natal lineage, which is where he is thought "really" to belong and to which he almost always returns as an operating member in adult life.

The association of proprietary rights with principles of descent-group membership in parts of Africa thus stands in contrast with the separation of proprietary rights from descent-group membership in parts of Oceania. From Oceania, also, we find some interesting examples of an association of proprietary rights and descent-group membership that differs from the way they are associated in the African examples. Palau in Micronesia (Barnett 1949) is best documented.

Palauan society is divided into a series of groups that are called matrilineal lineages in the literature; but I shall call them "houses." A man has proprietary rights in the labor and loyalty of his younger siblings and of his sister's children. He is ultimately responsible for financing their marriages and for underwriting their financial obligations. In the system of exchange, food, goods, and services are exchanged for money. Successful dealing in the exchange system is the basis of the social rank of the several houses in a community. When a man marries, he contracts to buy the sexual and domestic services of his wife, in return for which he pays money. His wife's brothers also supply him with goods and services, for which he must pay. Since control over the labor of his own children lies with his wife's brother, he must pay his wife's brother for the labor and services he gets from his children. However, for a price in money, he can contract with his wife's brother to take over the financial responsibility for his own children and the direct control of their labor and loyalty. If the children prove to be lazy and a liability rather than an asset, he can terminate the contract, and their maternal uncle must reassume financial responsibility for them. Otherwise, his children now work for him directly. Before, they operated as members of the house in which their maternal uncle operated as a member; now they operate as members of the house in which their father operates as a member. This arrangement terminates on the father's death (or his divorce or remarriage), and the children then revert to the control of their maternal uncle or of their eldest brother, if they have no maternal uncle. They may also arrange for someone to adopt them, the adopting father in turn contracting with the maternal uncle or elder brother for their services. Thus they can acquire a powerful financial sponsor, and in return they operate as members of their adoptive father's house. Each house is ideally headed by the eldest man in the direct line of matrilineal descent from its founder. Therefore, when a man becomes eligible to be head of the house to which he is ultimately tied by matrilineal descent, he leaves the service of his father or adoptive father and becomes head of the house of which his older brother and maternal uncle had been head before him. He acquires control of the labor and loyalty of the house's operating members, who may be the children of its female birthright members and who may also be the children and grandchildren of its male birthright members. There are occasions when there is no one in the female line descending from the founder who is of a suitable age and ability to assume headship of a house. A son of a birthright member may then be designated head of the house with the understanding that headship will revert to a birthright member later. The son who thus holds the headship in trust will have spent much of his life as an operating member of the house. He may even be simultaneously head of the house in which he is a birthright member.

The problem the Palauan houses posed for ethnographers was that Palauans talked about them in the abstract in terms of birthright membership, and in these terms they were matrilineal lineages; but census data provided information on current operating memberships, and in these terms the houses were nonunilineal lineages, varying in appearance from being predominantly matrilineal all the way to being predominantly patrilineal. If the Palauans were to discard their competition for rank through the manipulation of exchanges of money and services, their houses would then be unequivocal matrilineal lineages with a coincidence of birthright and operating memberships.

There is an obvious difference between the Palauan houses and those of the Okrika Ijo. Palauans preserve a unilineal birthright membership as the ultimate point of reference, but allow transactions in proprietary rights in persons to affect operating membership. The Orika Ijo do not bother to keep a birthright membership as a point of ultimate reference, transferring membership outright with the transfer of proprietary rights. This contrast shows the importance of examining the various kinds of rights people have in one another and in groups and of seeing how these rights are actually clustered in each ethnographic case. Failure to do so—from, I believe, ethnocentric assumptions about the association of descent, kinship, fatherhood, and proprietary rights—has severely limited the cogency of anthropological discussion about descent groups.

THE CONSTITUENTS OF DESCENT GROUPS

So far, I have dealt with descent groups only as aggregations of individuals. It is as such that anthropologists have usually dealt with them. But social groups, descent groups included, can have other groups rather than individuals as their immediate constituents.

The traditional Chinese lineages provide an example (Freedman 1958, 1966). A Chinese woman is without adult status in the family in which she was born. She is an adult in the family into which she marries. At marriage she is initiated into her husband's lineage and introduced to her new ancestors. The adults in these lineages consist of patrilineally related men and their wives, but not their sisters. In this respect, a Chinese lineage resembles what Murdock (1949:66) has called a "compromise kin group." He saw such groups as based on a rule of descent for one sex and a rule of residence in marriage for the other; and he conceived of them as strictly local groups. The Chinese lineages or lineage segments may or may not be discrete local groups. The membership even of lineage segments may be residentially somewhat scattered in a given region. But adult membership is based on patrilineal descent for men and on marriage for women. So much so that special "spinster houses" are provided in some areas to which unmarried women and divorced women must repair to die and with which memorial tablets for them are associated. They cannot have their tablets associated with their natal lineages. Murdock's emphasis on residence, I think, was somewhat beside the mark; he would better have emphasized marriage. But to place the emphasis on marriage suggests something else: that the constituents of Chinese lineages are families, which are linked patrilineally through their male heads.

The so-called patrilineal lineages of the Nuer in the Republic of the Sudan (Evans-Pritchard 1940) consist of local groups linked into lineages by putative patrilineal ties connecting their respective headmen. Membership in the local groups does not rest solely on patrilineal considerations. Here the descent groups have local groups as their immediate constituents, as Scheffler (1966) and Buchler and Selby (1968:74–75) have also observed.

The chiefdoms of Truk (Goodenough 1951) are composed of several matrilineal lineages. Each lineage is a corporation holding title to sections of ground within the territory of the chiefdom. One lineage holds a title to the entire space of the territory, as distinct from parcels of ground within it. This lineage theoretically founded the chiefdom by acquiring title to the space. It granted portions of it to the children of its men. Under matrilineal descent the children were not members of their fathers' lineage and became the founders of new local lineages. These new lineages held title to the portions of ground granted them but owed first fruits to the founding lineage in return for use of the space. Such a new lineage might, in turn, make grants of ground to the children of its men and receive first fruits from them in return for their use of the ground. The entire chiefdom was conceived as a set of matrilineal lineages linked through their founders by father-child ties to the original lineage, whose head was chief and titular "father" of them all. Thus a set of matrilineal descent groups were constituents of a larger "patrilineal" group, which was the chiefdom.[21]

CONCLUSION

I have by now traveled quite a distance into the complexities of descent groups. Starting with the simple motion of descent from a focal ancestor, I have examined some of the ways membership in descent groups may be restricted. If membership is an individual's right, then the composition of descent groups will be a reflection of the choices people have and of how they exercise them. Such descent groups cannot be unilineal. They may or may not overlap their memberships. If membership is an individual's duty, however, or if it is ascribed to him in some way, the resulting groups may be unilineal or not, depending on the principles governing ascription. These principles may involve jural rights or they may not, being a part of what is considered the order of nature. Finally, we saw that groups of various kinds, as well as individuals, may be the constituents of descent groups.

From this perspective, how are we to regard the existing conventional anthropological view of descent groups as being composed of individuals and as being of three basic kinds: patrilineal, matrilineal, and cognatic? If this view appears inadequate, how are we to regard the many theoretical propositions that take these conventional anthropological categories for granted?

21. Some readers may object to using the adjective "patrilineal" to describe this larger group. Yet it consists of units that are descended from an ancestral unit through a chain of father-child connections.

3. Sibling and Cousin

"THE SCIENTIFIC significance of kinship systems was first appreciated by Morgan in what is perhaps the most original and brilliant single achievement in the history of anthropology." Thus, almost eighty years after Morgan's (1871) great work, Murdock (1949: 91) introduced what represented the next global comparative study of the ways people categorize kin relationships. In the same paragraph Murdock added, "No other anthropological topic, in all probability, has been the beneficiary of so much creative effort." Anthropological interest in the subject has continued unabated in the twenty years since Murdock wrote.

In his account of the Iroquois, Morgan (1851:81) observed that in "computing degrees of consanguinity . . . no distinction was made between the lineal and collateral lines, either in the ascending or descending series." His genius saw the possibility that such different ways of classifying kinsmen might be functionally tied to different forms of family and kingroup organization. Murdock's work confirmed the validity of Morgan's insight beyond further dispute. Morgan's ideas regarding the meaning of the functional linkage have fared less well, but the fact of functional linkage can no longer be denied.

Because of the great attention given the subject, anthropologists have developed a fairly extensive technical vocabulary and several typologies for systems of kinship terms. This technical apparatus for describing, typing, and comparing kinship terminologies is my present topic.

Morgan (1877:403) distinguished between what he called "descriptive" and "classificatory" terminologies. A descriptive terminology did not group any relationship within the elementary conjugal family with any relationship outside of it under a single label. A classificatory terminology did do this, denoting relationships inside and outside the elementary conjugal family by the same words.[1] Thus, the kinship terminology of the Lapps is descriptive in that it has separate terms for the kintypes we call father, mother, brother, sister, son, daughter, husband, and wife; whereas the Lakalai of New Britain have a classificatory terminology in that they refer to siblings and parallel cousins[2] by the same terms indiscriminately and do the same with children and parallel nephews

1. This characterizes the distinction between descriptive and classificatory terminologies as Morgan and others after him have made it in practice. Morgan actually conceived of it somewhat differently. With classificatory systems, he wrote (1877:403–404), "consanguinei are never described, but are classified into categories, irrespective of their nearness or remoteness in degree to *Ego;* and the same term of relationship is applied to all the persons in the same category." With descriptive terms, "consanguinei are described either by the primary terms of relationship or a combination of these terms, thus making the relationship of each person specific. Thus we say brother's son, father's brother, and father's brother's son." In his developmental scheme this had originally characterized the kinship system of "the Aryan, Semitic, and Uralian families, which came in with monogamy. A small amount of classification was subsequently introduced by the invention of common terms; but the earliest form of the system, of which the Erse and Scandinavian are typical, was purely descriptive." Thus he conceived of a descriptive system as one that accurately expressed degrees of consanguinity, while classificatory systems ignored degrees of consanguinity. "The radical difference between the two systems resulted from plural marriages in the group in one case, and from single marriages between single pairs in the other."

2. Parallel cousins are the children of siblings of same sex (the children of two brothers or the children of two sisters), while cross-cousins are the children of siblings of opposite sex. Similarly, a parallel nephew or niece is the child of a sibling of ego's sex (a brother's child, if ego is male), and a cross-nephew or niece is the child of a sibling of opposite sex to ego. Kay (1965) has provided a useful generalization of the cross/parallel distinction.

and nieces. In Truk, there are no terms that refer only to relationships within the elementary conjugal family.[3]

In 1909 Kroeber observed that from another standpoint all kinship terms are classificatory in that they designate classes or categories of kin relationship. There are several possible criteria, he said, for differentiating among kinsmen and ordering them into classes. To use all these criteria simultaneously would create more distinctions than are practically needed and more than can readily be learned or proficiently used in a kindred of any size. The difference between Morgan's descriptive and classificatory terminologies, and the differences among various classificatory terminologies themselves, can be understood as resulting from the different ways people have selected from among these criteria in order to classify their kinsmen. If certain criteria are used in combination, then each of the basic relationships within the elementary family will be distinguished from one another and from all other relationships; otherwise, they will not be. The criteria given by Kroeber (1909: 78–79) were eight in number as follows: (1) "the difference between persons of the same and of separate generation," (2) "the difference between lineal and collateral relationship," (3) "difference of age within one generation," (4) "the sex of the relative," (5) "the sex of the speaker," (6) "the sex of the person through whom [the] relationship exists," (7) "the distinction of blood relatives from connections by marriage," (8) "the condition of life of the person through whom the relationship exists." These criteria were subsequently increased to nine by Murdock (1949:101–106) as "generation," "sex," "affinity," "collaterality," "bifurcation" (Kroeber's sixth criterion) "polarity" (the addition to Kroeber's list), "relative age," "speaker's sex," and "decedence" (Kroeber's eighth criterion).

The first six of his nine criteria in combination, Murdock (1949: 101) observed, will have the effect of separating out each relation-

---

3. Such relationships can be readily denoted, but require descriptive phrases, such as "one only our 'father' and one only our 'mother'," in which "father" and "mother" are now understood to refer to relationships within the conjugal family as distinct from their ordinarily wide range of denotation.

ship in the elementary conjugal family in a manner corresponding to English terminological usage. Any relationship thus distinguished by these six major criteria when used in combination he called a "kintype." And any term that denotes only one kintype he called a "denotative" term, whereas any term that can denote more than one kintype he called a "classificatory" term, in keeping with Morgan's usage. Like Kroeber, he saw the differences among kinship terminologies as a result of how these nine criteria are selectively recognized and ignored. The nine criteria, he said (1949:106), "yield most if not all of the known variations in kinship nomenclature." The problem to which he then addressed himself was to develop and test a postulate regarding the conditions under which people were more or less likely to recognize or ignore each of the six major criteria.

These criteria also were used, in part, as the basis for a typology of kinship systems by Lowie (1929). I shall reserve consideration of his and other typologies by Spier (1925) and Murdock (1949) until my last lecture.

Nearly twenty years ago, when I was writing an ethnographic account of social organization in Truk (1951), I tried to explicate Trukese kinship terminology in such a way that an American reader could understand the principles by which all kinsmen in Truk are categorized. What does one have to know about A and B in Truk in order to say that A properly refers to B as *semey* rather than as *iney, pwiiy, feefiney, mwááni, neyi, éésey,* or *pwúnúwey?* This is what I wanted to communicate. I treated these particular Trukese terms as a system of terms, and then dealt with some additional ones as "special" terms.

It occurred to me to ask myself why I regarded the former set of terms as forming a system and what I called special terms as outside of that system. It then struck me that the terms I had grouped together in a system all designated classes of kintypes that did not overlap and were complementary, whereas the classes of kintypes designated by the special terms overlapped those designated by the terms I had intuitively treated as a system. To state it another way, the classes of kintypes making up the designata of terms in the system could all be discriminated from one another with reference to the same set of criteria or discriminating variables. The differences among these classes were functions of the same set of considerations.

From this observation, I got the idea for the kind of descriptive semantics that has become known as "componential analysis," an idea that Floyd Lounsbury was independently evolving for himself and that he and I coincidentally published in the same number of *Language,* one dedicated to Kroeber (Lounsbury 1956, Goodenough 1956a). Because what I have to present are some of the things I have learned from this kind of analysis, it will be necessary for me to describe it briefly.[4]

COMPONENTIAL ANALYSIS

In the usage of Morris (1938), a linguistic expression may be said to *designate* a class of concepts or images. It may be said to *denote* a specific image or subclass of images within the class on any one occasion of its use. And it may be said to *signify* the criteria by which specific images or concepts are to be included or excluded from the class of images or concepts that the expression designates. What is signified consists of the definitive attributes of the class, the ideational components from which the class is conceptually formed. Componential analysis is a method for forming and testing hypotheses about what words signify.

In following the method, we make a record of the specific images or concepts that informants indicate an expression may denote.[5] Our next task is to find a set of definitive attributes that will account for what informants have said may and may not be denoted by the expression and that, by the same token, predict what informants will say may be denoted by the expression in the future. We do this

4. For brief up-to-date accounts of componential analysis, see Goodenough (1967, 1968), and for a fuller and more technical account, illustrated with reference to American English kinship terms, see Goodenough (1965a). See also Lounsbury (1964a).

5. Expressions do not denote things but images of things. Things serve as material representations of the images (or of concepts of them constructed in the act of perceiving them) and are *tokens* of the class of such images designated by the expression. The observer makes a record of his images of the material representations of his informant's images.

by a combination of two operations. One is to inspect the denotata, as we have recorded them, for common attributes. The other and more crucial operation is to contrast the set of the expression's denotata with sets of denotata of other expressions.

The English kinship term *aunt* provides an example.[6] As I use the term, I would list for it such denotata as mother's sister, father's sister, mother's or father's half-sister, mother's brother's (or half-brother's) wife, father's brother's (or half-brother's) wife. By performing the two operations indicated, we might arrive at the following componential definition of what *aunt* signifies: any relative by blood or marriage who is simultaneously A: female, B: two degrees of genealogical distance from ego, C: not lineal, D: in a senior generation, and E: not connected by a marital tie in other than the senior generation of the relationship (cf. Goodenough 1965a).

In this way the several conceptually discrete or disjunctive denotata have been brought together in a conceptually unified or conjunctive set. They form a class or category that can be described as a product of the combination of the several definitive attributes. That they serve as definitive attributes in this case is evident from our observing that to vary any one of them results in a judgment that *aunt* is impermissible as a term of reference. Vary attribute A above (the relative's sex), and *uncle* becomes the appropriate term. *Great aunt* becomes appropriate if we vary B, *grandmother* if we vary C, *niece* if we vary D, and *wife's aunt* or *husband's aunt* if we vary E. In this way we can verify the adequacy of a componential definition.

In this example, the definitive attributes forming the significatum of *aunt* are values of conceptual variables whose other values form the significata of other terms in English kinship terminology. To have to use five different variables in a componential definition of *aunt* may seem cumbersome as against the short exhaustive list of denotata. But if the same variables account for other English terms, a considerable advantage has been gained by using componential definitions. They not only describe the significata of single words, they also show how the significata of different words may be related to one another.

6. This example and the discussion based upon it are taken from an earlier account of mine (Goodenough 1967), which is followed almost *verbatim*.

In the case of *aunt, uncle, nephew, niece,* and so on, the respective significata differ as functions of the common set of defining variables. The respective designata, moreover, are mutually exclusive and complementary. We seem to be dealing with some kind of conceptual or ideal space—call it a genealogical one—that has been partitioned into cells by a set of defining variables, each cell being represented by a linguistic label. All the labels designating the complementary cells of a conceptual space (or domain, as it is frequently called) form an ordered array or terminological system, one in which the significatum of each label indicates in what respects its designatum differs from the designata of other labels.

As the example of the English term *aunt* reveals, the criteria that taken together define what English kinship terms signify are not unlike Kroeber's old list of eight criteria of kinship. But the analyses of different kinship terminologies that I have done over the past dozen years show that Kroeber's criteria are not in themselves adequate to the task of accounting for the significata of kinship terms, although they are an important contribution to that end. What I have learned makes it possible to re-examine Kroeber's and Murdock's criteria as to their actual utility, and to refine them and expand upon them. The results of such re-examination are my present topic.

GENEALOGICAL SPACE

We begin with a consideration of genealogical space, for a terminology that involves no properties of genealogical space is not a kinship terminology. What I am calling genealogical space is composed of a chain of connections between two persons as ego and alter. These connections consist either of one or more parent-child links, in what can be called a consanguineal chain, or of one or more marital ties, or of both together. A consanguineal link is conventionally represented by a solid line and a marital tie by an equals sign (Figure 1).

Figure 1. Ego (E) is the sibling of alter's (A's) spouse.

Given an ego, an alter, and some mediating kinsmen through whom they are connected by some combination of parent-child links and marital ties, the following represent the major considerations by which kin relationships may be differentiated:

1. properties of the genealogical space between ego and alter (e.g., presence or absence of marital ties);
2. properties of the genealogical space or particular positions in it relative to ego or alter (e.g., presence or absence of a marital tie involving alter);
3. properties of ego (e.g., sex);
4. properties of alter (e.g., sex);
5. properties of ego relative to alter (e.g., similarity of sex, relative age);
6. properties of a mediating or linking kinsman in the relationship (e.g., sex of alter's linking parent);
7. properties of a mediating kinsman relative to properties of ego, of alter, or of another mediating kinsman (e.g., the similarity of their sex, their relative age);
8. properties of particular positions in the genealogical space without reference to whether they are occupied by ego, by alter, or by a mediating kinsman (e.g., sex of the senior terminus of the consanguineal chain between ego and alter).

With these in mind, we may now consider each of Kroeber's and Murdock's criteria in turn.

CONSANGUINITY AND AFFINITY

Among the most important properties of genealogical space are the presence or absence of consanguineal links and marital ties. These were what Kroeber and Murdock were referring to by their criterion of "affinity." There are actually several possible criteria here.

First is the simple presence/absence of a marital (affinal) tie in the relationship between ego and alter. The Könkämä Lapps of Sweden, for example, distinguish all kin relationships in which a marital tie is present from all those in which there is none (Goodenough 1964).

A second criterion is the number of marital ties. Some terminologies distinguish relationships in which there are two marital ties from those in which there is one, and the latter from those in which there are none. The Könkämä Lapps make limited use of this criterion in conjunction with the extended use of the simple presence of a marital tie.

A variation on this is to distinguish relationships in which there is an odd number of marital ties between ego and alter from those in which there is not an odd number. The result is that relationships with two marital ties are classed with those in which there are none by contrast with those in which there is one or a higher odd number. The people of Moala in Fiji use this criterion in combination with another one (Goodenough 1968), as do the Kariera of Australia (see Appendix).

A fourth criterion is the location of the marital tie in the genealogical space without reference to the location of ego and alter. In common American usage, for example, if ego and alter are in different generations in the relationships E=X——A and E——X=A, a marital tie makes a difference if it is in the junior generation but is ignored if it is in the senior generation. Thus, the spouses of my aunts and uncles are also my aunts and uncles (the marital tie being ignored), but the aunts and uncles of my spouse are not my aunts and uncles. I must refer to the latter by a descriptive phrase, such as "my uncle by marriage," or "my wife's aunt."

This last criterion seems to be used widely in the world. The presence of a marital tie in the youngest generation of the relationship is a criterion for differentiating among kinsmen used by the Lakalai of New Britain, for example. Whether there is an odd or even number of such marital ties makes a difference in kinship usage in Moala, Fiji, but the presence of other marital ties is irrelevant (Goodenough 1968). Relationships of the type shown in Figure 2, moreover, are usually classed as altogether different, the difference, again, being in the location of the marital tie in a generation senior as against one junior to the generation of ego and alter.

Figure 2. Step-siblings contrasted with co-parents-in-law.

A fifth criterion is the location of a marital tie with reference to ego or alter. Thus the Kalmuk distinguish relationships in which there is an ego-centered marital tie (E=X———A) from those in which there is not such a tie. At the same time, they independently distinguish relationships in which there is an alter-centered marital tie (E———X=A) from those in which there is not such a tie. In this way they produce an exceedingly large corpus of terms for relatives by marriage, in which usage is largely nonreciprocal. They further complicate matters by ignoring ego-centric marital ties when ego is female and alter is junior to ego.[7]

Paralleling the presence or absence of a marital tie is the simple presence or absence of a consanguineal link (or chain) between ego and alter. This may be relevant when relationships between spouses (E=A) and co-spouses in polygyny (E=X=A) are distinguished from all other relationships in which there is also a marital tie.

The number of consanguineal chains between ego and alter may also be significant. The Lakalai of New Britain distinguish relationships in which there is more than one consanguineal chain between ego and alter (E———X=X———A) from those in which there is not more than one, for example. And the Könkämä Lapps distinguish affinal relationships with two consanguineal chains from those with one (Goodenough 1964).

This last criterion and the one preceding it (presence of a consanguineal link or chain between ego and alter) reveal that consanguinity and affinity are not necessarily two values of the same variable, although they can often be construed as such. With one consanguineal chain, there may be one, two, or no marital ties between ego and alter; with two consanguineal chains there may be one, two, or three marital ties between ego and alter.

GENERATION

Kroeber's and Murdock's criterion of generation also breaks down into several criteria.

---

7. Data on the Kalmuk for this analysis come from the accounts by Aberle (1953) and Adelman (1954).

First is generation distance. Many terminologies distinguish relationships by the number of generations there are between ego and alter and make no further distinctions, especially among remoter generations. The Lakalai illustrate. They have a single term for a kinsman five generations distant, another term for any kinsman four generations distant, a term for a kinsman three generations distant, and one for a kinsman two generations distant. These terms are used without regard to who is the senior and who the junior, without regard to sex, or anything else. Such further distinctions are added only with reference to kinsmen who are less than two generations removed.[8]

Another way to handle the idea of generation is to distinguish kin relationships where ego and alter are in the same generation from those in which they are in different generations (Kroeber's original distinction). The people of Truk do this, making no distinctions of generation distance at all (Goodenough 1956a). They distinguish relatives in other than ego's generation only according to whether their generation is senior or junior to ego's.

Generation can be handled in yet another way: by distinguishing relatives in odd generations in relation to ego's (or to the junior party's) from relatives in even generations. Thus ego and his grandparents and grandchildren are in one generational bin, while his parents and children are in aother. Names for the so-called sections of the Kariera of Australia (see Appendix) provide a well known example (Brown 1913); and their kinship terminology has been analyzed by Romney and Epling (1958) and Reid (1967) with this as a criterion of classification.[9]

---

8. Aberle (1967) has treated cases in which at least some kintypes in the second ascending generation are equated with at least some kintypes in the second descending generation (without involvement of any kintypes in ego's generation) as the weakest form of "alternate generation terminology." From the point of view presented here, such equations result from the use of degree of generation distance as a criterion without concurrent use of generation seniority. Alternate-generation terminology may also result from the differentiation of odd from even generations without further consideration of degree of distance or of generation seniority. Most of Aberle's examples do not seem to qualify as alternate-generation terminology in this latter sense.

9. My own analysis of Kariera kinship terminology (see Appendix) differs from the analysis of Romney and Epling (1958) and of Reid (1967) in that

COLLATERALITY

A lineal relationship is one in which the consanguineal chain between ego and alter is composed entirely of parent-child links such that one terminus of the chain is an ancestor of the other terminus

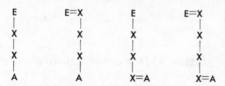

Figure 3. Examples of lineal (noncollateral) relationships between ego (E) and alter (A). The positions of ego and alter may be reversed.

(Figure 3). A collateral relationship is one in which neither terminus of the consaguineal chain is ancestral to the other (Figure 4).

Some kinship terminologies simply distinguish lineal from collateral relationships without concern for degrees of collateral distance. This is apparently what Kroeber and Murdock had in mind for their criterion of collaterality. Many societies distinguish degree of collaterality (collateral distance) as well.

In a collateral relationship there are two lines of parent-child links descending from a common ancestor, one leading to ego and the other to alter. The number of parent-child links in the shorter of the two lines determines collateral distance. When the shorter line has only one parent-child link, ego and alter are first-degree

---

I find section membership unsatisfactory as a criterion of kinship classification. It works well if one does the analysis for a male ego only (as did Romney and Epling) or for a female ego only, but it does not work for both together. Furthermore, its use as a criterion results in an unnecessary number of terms with disjunctive definitions and destroys the integrity of closed sets of reciprocal terms, an integrity that the rules of componential analysis require us to preserve (Goodenough 1965a, 1967). But the distinction between odd and even generations serves as a necessary criterion, at least implicitly, in my analysis, too. The patrilineal moieties, whose combination with odd and even generations account for the named sections, also fail to account for the sets of denotata and patterns of reciprocation of Kariera kinship terms.

collaterals; when it has two parent-child links, they are second-degree collaterals; and so on (Figure 4).

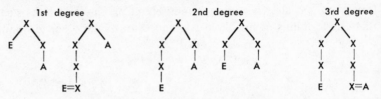

Figure 4. Degrees of collaterality.

Degree of collaterality figures in American kinship terminology prominently as a criterion for distinguishing categories of kin. We make a basic distinction between all relatives who are less than two degrees of collateral distance and those who are two or more degrees distant. The former set is subdivided by other criteria, but any kinsman in the latter set is one's *cousin*. We introduce degree of collaterality further when we speak of *first, second,* and *third* cousins (keeping track of generation by reference to the number of *times removed*).

SEX AND BIFURCATION

Murdock and Kroeber saw three criteria involving sex: the sex of alter, the sex of ego, and the sex of a mediating (linking) kinsman in the genealogical chain between ego and alter. This last Murdock, following Lowie, called the criterion of bifurcation. The Aymara have two terms for sibling, for example, one for a sibling with the same father as ego and another for a sibling with the same mother as ego. Either term may be used for a sibling with whom ego shares the same persons as father and mother.[10]

There are other uses of sex that were not noted by Murdock and Kroeber. Often what matters is the sex of the senior party to the relationship, who may be either alter or ego. Thus the Kariera of Australia (Brown 1913) have four terms for grandparents and

10. I am indebted to John T. Cole for this example. It represents one of the few cases of which I have record in which the sex of a linking relative serves as a criterion of differentiation among kinsmen. Most examples cited as illustrations of bifurcation, as thus defined, turn out to involve other uses of sex as a criterion.

grandchildren as follows: *maeli,* father's father, son's son (of a man) and son's daughter (of a man); *kabali,* father's mother, son's son (of a woman), and son's daughter (of a woman); *tami,* mother's father, daughter's son (of a man), daughter's daughter (of a man); *kandari,* mother's mother, daughter's son (of a woman), daughter's daughter (of a woman). From each term one knows the sex of the senior relative but not that of the junior relative. The same criterion is used frequently in connection with the terms for cross-aunts and uncles and cross-nephews and nieces. A Lakalai refers to his (or her) maternal uncle by the same term he uses back for his sister's son and daughter; and a paternal aunt uses the same term for her brother's son and daughter that they both use for her (as shown in relationships B and C in Figure 5 below). Many cases of what superficially appear as if sex of ego were being used as a criterion turn out on closer examination to involve sex of the senior party. The grandparent and grandchild terms of the Könkämä Lapps are a case in point (Goodenough 1964).

Sex of the junior party (but not the senior) is sometimes a criterion in relationships having a marital tie in the junior generation. Thus a Lakalai man refers to both his father-in-law and mother-in-law by a term they use back for him, and a woman uses a different term reciprocally with her parents-in-law. Greenberg (1966:105) has said, "Whenever there are two terms differing in generation which are true reciprocals, or there is one which is a self-reciprocal term with two referents and one involves the sex of the speaker in its definition and the other does not, it is always the term of lower generational reference which contains the sex of the speaker in its definition." That is, the sex of the senior party is always the sex that is distinguished. He seems to be correct for relationships in which there is no marital tie in the junior generation. But in the latter event, as the Lakalai testify, the reverse may hold true.

The sex of alter relative to the sex of ego appears frequently as a criterion.[11] In the kinship terminology of Pidgin English, as this language is spoken in the New Guinea area, the word *barata* (from

11. Not mentioned by Kroeber or Murdock, this criterion was explicitly recognized by Davis and Warner (1937) in a paper stimulated by Kroeber's earlier one.

English *brother*) refers to either the brother of a man or the sister of a woman, whereas the word *sisa* or *susa* (from English *sister*) refers to either the brother of a woman or the sister of a man (Murphy 1954:26). Here, if one hears that A is B's *barata*, one knows that A and B are of the same sex; but one may not know what that sex is, especially if, as among the Lakalai, there are no sex differences in personal names.[12] The people of Truk use this criterion, having a single term for generation mates of the same sex, but they combine it with the criterion of sex of alter for generation mates of opposite sex, having one term for the male kinsman of a woman and another for the female kinsman of a man (Goodenough 1951:94).[13]

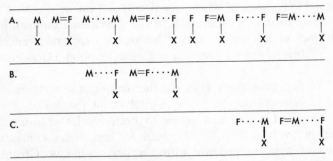

Figure 5. Diagram of relationships covered by reciprocal sets A, B, C of Lakalai kinship terms. M = male; F = female; X = person of either sex; horizontal dotted line indicates collateral relationship in same generation of indefinite degree; vertical line indicates a parent-child connection.

Consideration of similarity and difference of sex can apply to positions in the consanguineal chain between ego and alter. Thus in relationships in which ego and alter are one generation distant and in which there are no marital ties in the junior generation of the relationship, the Lakalai distinguish three reciprocal sets of terms, which we may label A, B, and C. Their respective ranges of

12. See my account (1965b) of personal names among the Lakalai.
13. Nerlove and Romney (1967) discuss the various distinctions that are possible for siblings and the relative frequency of their occurrence.

denotata are given in Figure 5. Inspection of these denotata reveals that the relationships in set A are set off from those in sets B and C by virtue of the presence in B and C of a sex difference between the consanguineally related pair in the genealogical chain in the first ascending generation of the relationship (the generation immediately senior to that of the junior party to the relationship). The sex of the linking parent of the junior party does not in itself account for the data. In set B, for example, the linking parent may be male or female; the constant is the difference of sex.

Consideration of the similarity and difference of sex of pairs of mediating relatives prepares us to understand the terminology of Moala in Fiji (Sahlins 1962). Here, according to my analysis (Goodenough 1968), a distinction is based on the number of coeval pairs of opposite sex in the generations in the genealogical chain other than in the youngest generation. To this number is added the number of marital ties in the youngest generation. If the combined number is odd, ego and alter are in one kind of relationship; if the combined number is even, they are in the other kind of relationship (Figure 6). It sounds horribly complicated, but in reckoning to a distant relative it is very simple if you use a common relative whose relationship to each of you is already known. Then the rule is that the even of my even is my even, as is the odd of my odd; but the even of my odd is my odd, as is the odd of my even. As marriages take place or new children are borne, one need only look to see whether or not the new relative adds a marital tie that counts or a coeval sex difference that matters. If one thinks of similarity and difference of sex as involving notions of symmetry and asymmetry, and if one thinks of oddness and evenness as involving the same notions of symmetry and asymmetry; then the Moala terminology becomes one in which symmetry appears at a more abstract level as an underlying criterion of classification.

The Moala case is especially interesting, because it represents a distribution of kinship terms that anthropologists have assumed made sense only given the presence of unilineal moieties that exchanged women in marriage. In an extended review of Sahlins' book, Groves (1963b) makes this the hub of his critique, arguing that Sahlins has not understood his Moala data correctly and has failed to appreciate that he is dealing with a pattern of marital exchanges or alliances between sets of agnates. Groves is a victim

Even Relationships

Odd Relationships

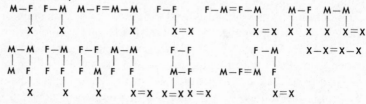

Figure 6. Patterns of odd and even relationship in Moala kinship terminology. For M, read "male," for F, "female," for =, "is married to," for horizontal line, "is sibling of," for vertical line, "is child or parent of." What count are sex differences among coeval consanguineal pairs except in the youngest generation and marital ties in the youngest generation.

of his lack of alternative models for making sense of what Sahlins presented. No moieties and no moiety-like exchanges of wives between agnatic (patrilineal) groups are required to make sense of the Moala kinship terminology. The notions of odd and even in conjunction with the notions of sex difference and marriage are all the Moalans need to find their way around the kinship landscape readily and easily. Yalman (1962) has called attention to the existence of similar kinship terminology in Ceylon in the absence of unilinear descent groups. The kinship terminology he gives there and in a subsequent publication (1967) follows the same basic pattern as that of Moala and can be analyzed in terms of the same odd-even patterning of sex differences among coeval pairs in other than the youngest generation plus marital ties in the youngest generation.

If this odd-even approach leaves you unhappy because its application in the way I have described seems to be strange and unfamiliar, I call attention to a similar phenomenon in Cayuga Iroquois phonology, reported by Lounsbury (1963). In Cayuga for every vowel and consonant there are two modes of pronunciation. One mode is always associated with the first, third, fifth, and subsequent odd syllables of a word, the other mode with the second, fourth, sixth, and subsequent even syllables. If a prefix is added, what was the first syllable becomes the second, and the pronunciation of every syllable in the word flips from the odd to the even or from the even to the odd mode, accordingly. For someone not used to such a manner of speaking, this must seem strange indeed; but after a little practice, doing it becomes "second nature." The simplicity of cultural forms must be measured by the ease with which people learn to work with them as the first cultural forms to which they are exposed, not by the strangeness with which they strike people who have already learned to behave in other ways instead.

Moala is not unique. Odd–even reckoning of the number of sex differences among coeval collateral pairs in the genealogical chain together with the number of marital ties is also applicable to the kinship terminology of the Kariera of Australia, according to my analysis of the data reported by Radcliffe-Brown (Brown 1913). In this case one must keep odd and even generations in mind as well. A basic distinction cross-cutting the generations is between two classes of relationship that do not correspond to moiety or section membership. The distinction rests on the odd versus even number resulting from the number of sex differences among coeval collateral pairs in other than terminal even generations (as against terminal odd ones) added to the number of marital ties in terminal even generations. In this, the junior party is taken as the point of reference. Thus, if the parties to the relationship are two generations apart, both are in terminal even generations; but if they are one generation apart, only the junior party is in a terminal even generation. In the Appendix, I present a full account of the data and a componential analysis of the Kariera kinship terminology.

Even this does not exhaust the possible uses to which the idea of similarity of sex can be put. The Kariera terminology is susceptible of another interpretation in which the basic distinction cross-cutting the generations is accomplished by something other than the considerations just described. Here the significant thing is a sex difference between parent-child links in the genealogical chain. In the Kariera case, it involves the number of father-daughter and/ or mother-son links descending from even to odd generations in the genealogical chain. Cross-sex links descending from odd to even generations do not count. One then adds the number of marital ties in even generations. If the sum is even, ego and alter are in one type of basic relationship; if it is odd, they are in the other (cf. Kay 1965). Again the junior generation is the generation of reference for distinguishing odd from even generations. As in the other mode of reckoning, all one has to do is start from some known relationship that is odd or even. Every subsequent birth or marriage then either flips to the opposite or not depending on whether it creates a cross-sex, parent-child link or a marital tie that counts.

Another use of sex is illustrated by the kinship terminology of the Kalmuk Mongols, described by Aberle (1953) and Adelman (1954) and analyzed in part by Romney (1965). It is an example of what has been called an Omaha type of terminology in that cross-cousins are classed with senior relatives (such as aunts and uncles) on the maternal side and are classed with junior relatives (such as nephews and nieces) on the paternal side. The Kalmuk divide consanguineal kinsmen into four major types: *tör'lmud* (sg. *tör'l*) with many subcategories, *nakhtsanar* (sg. *nakhtsa*), *zeener* (sg. *zee*), and *bölner* (sg. *böl*). They fall into three reciprocal sets in that one is *tör'l* to one's *tör'l*, one is *zee* to one's *nakhtsa* and *nakhtsa* to one's *zee*, and one is *böl* to one's *böl*. These three reciprocal sets are diagramed in Figure 7.

What clearly distinguishes them from one another is the presence as against the absence of female-linking relatives in the genealogical chain between ego and alter. *Tör'l-tör'l* relationships (type I) are those in which there are no female links between ego and alter. Ego and alter may be male or female. This set includes ego's mother and his father's sister, but excludes his mother's sister. Among his first cousins it includes only ego's father's brother's children. *Nakhtsa-zee* relationships (type II) are those in which there are one or more female links in only one line of ascent in the genealogical chain between ego and alter. The line of ascent without links is regarded as senior to the one with female links. Ego's mother's brother's children, together with his mother's brother

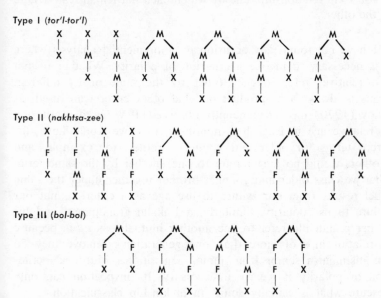

Figure 7. Three types of consanguineal relationship among the Kalmuk Mongols. F = female, M = male, X = male or female.

and mother's sister, are among his *nakhtsanar;* and his father's sister's children and sister's children are among his *zeener. Böl-böl* relationships (type III) are those in which there are one or more female links in each of the two lines of ascent in the genealogical chain between ego and alter. Ego's mother's sister's children ́are among his *bölner.*

POLARITY AND RECIPROCITY

Attaching great importance to what he called the criterion of polarity, Murdock has written (1949:104):

> The *criterion of polarity,* the last of the six major criteria for differentiating kinship terminology, arises from the sociological fact that it requires two persons to constitute a social relation-

ship. Linguistic recognition of this criterion produces two terms for a kin relationship, one by which each participant can denote the other.

I have not found any occasion in componential analysis where it is necessary to invoke a criterion of polarity. Whether or not two relatives refer to each other by the same or by different terms is always a by-product of what other criteria are used, as Aaby (1970) has independently observed. If we used a criterion of relative age in English terminology, then we would have different terms for older and younger brother, for example, and brothers would no longer refer to one another by the same term. That we class older and younger brother together under the same label results from our failure to use age as a criterion, not our failure to use polarity. Similarly, a Lakalai grandparent and his or her grandchild refer to one another mutually as *tubu,* because in relationships of more than one generation's remove they do not distinguish senior from junior generations. Murdock's criterion of polarity is clearly unnecessary. Its invocation can only obscure what is actually going on in kinship classification.

Murdock (1949:104, fn. 15) equated his "polarity" with what Kroeber (1909:80, fn. 1) referred to as "reciprocity." But Kroeber clearly meant something other than what Murdock meant by polarity. He had reference to the degree to which relationships are seen as mutual, in that for every alter, ego is an alter in the same relationship, whether they use the same or different terms for one another. As two distinct concepts, polarity and reciprocity are worthy of attention, however useless they may be as criteria of kinship classification.

Picking up from Kroeber, Aberle (1967:263) has distinguished between a "closed, polarized set" of kinship terms and a "closed, nonpolarized set." In the case of the Lakalai term *tubu,* to which I have just referred, we are dealing with a closed, nonpolarized set of relationships. The set is closed in that for every relationship in which ego uses the term alter uses it back, and ego uses it for alters who use it for him. It is nonpolarized in that those ego refers to as *tubu* do not use a different term back. The Trukese terms *mwááni* (male sibling of a woman) and *feefiney* (female sibling of a man) form a closed, polarized set—closed in that every alter for whom ego uses *mwááni* uses *feefiney* back, and *vice versa,* and polarized in that alter always uses back whichever term is not used by ego. The phenomenon of closure was what Kroeber had in mind when he spoke of reciprocity, and it is in this sense that I speak of reciprocal terms or reciprocal sets of terms in this chapter.[14]

Why some relationships are not polarized terminologically and others are is an intriguing question, regardless of the criteria of kinship classification by which polarization is or is not achieved. Aberle (1967:264) suggests that relationships that are terminologically polarized are felt to be significantly asymmetrical in some way, whereas nonpolarized relationships are felt to be essentially symmetrical. In keeping with this would be a hypothesis that in societies whose kinship terminology distinguishes older from younger brother, there is something asymmetrical in their relationship, such as the older having considerable authority over the younger; whereas in societies where the same term is used for older and younger brother, their relationship is felt to be symmetrical, neither having much authority over the other, for example, and both playing similar roles vis-à-vis other members of the family.

Such considerations take us beyond my topic. What concerns us now is that polarity and reciprocity are not criteria of kinship classification, but are significant facts about kinship that result from the criteria employed.

AGE AND SENIORITY

I have now dealt with all but two of Kroeber's and Murdock's criteria. The criterion of relative age requires no extended comment. Age distinctions can be applied to sibling pairs or to any pair of generation mates in the chain between ego and alter. Relative age is frequently applied to the coeval pairs in the generation

14. Closed sets may involve more than one or two terms, as Kroeber and Aberle have recognized. Thus, in English the terms *father* and *mother* together reciprocate the terms *son* and *daughter,* taken together. The result is a closed, polarized set of relationships, as we recognize with the pair of cover-terms *parent* and *child.* Finding the terms that taken together encompass closed or reciprocal sets of relationships is of great importance in componential analysis (Goodenough 1967).

immediately senior to the youngest one in the relationship. Among the Lakalai, for example, the term *tete* is used for ego's father, but his father's older male generation mate is *tete-uru* ("big father") and his father's younger male generation mate is *tete-bisi* or *te-bisi* ("little father"). The Könkämä Lapps make the same distinctions, but use the unrelated terms *ačče* for father, *akke* for father's older, coeval, male consanguine, and *čæcce* for father's younger, coeval, male consanguine (Pehrson 1957). Relative age or birth order may also be used with reference to the coeval pair closest to the apical ancestor, as when terminological distinctions are made between senior and junior lines of descent from a common ancestor.

The idea of seniority applies more commonly to generations, of course, than to birth order within generations. The distinction between parent and child is universally made, and the more general distinction between senior and junior generations is commonly added to the criterion of generation distance.

Taken somewhat more abstractly as a criterion of temporal priority, seniority can apply to priority of marriage among co-wives in polygyny. The Lakalai term I glossed above as "little father" is used not only for one's father's younger brothers and his younger male cousins; it is used for one's step-father as well. Thus it refers to any "father" subsequent to one's principal "father" by any manner of temporal reckoning.

DECEDENCE

Last of Murdock's "nine criteria" is decedence (Kroeber's "condition of life" of a linking relative). Murdock cites it only in connection with the change in marital status of a brother's wife relative to ego when ego's brother dies and ego is eligible or expected to marry her. The Huichol, for example, have a term for a man's wife's sister and brother's wife (used reciprocally back by a woman); but a man uses a different term for a wife's sister after his wife dies, if the wife's sister is then married to another man and ineligible as a replacement for the deceased wife (Grimes and Grimes 1962). Murdock regards this criterion as "not itself of great consequence" (1949:106). Actually, I think that what is referred to here is of considerable interest and may illuminate some of the more perplexing problems in the ethnographic description of kinship terminology.

We are used to seeing kinship terms as referring to classes or categories of relationship, some of which are broadly and some of which are narrowly defined, depending on the criteria employed. It is largely from this point of view that I have been discussing them. We are not used to thinking of kinship terms as designating titles or offices whose occupancy is governed by rules of succession. Yet this is what the principle of decedence seems to imply.

Schneider has reported that on Yap in Micronesia a kinship term I shall gloss as "father" is used for only one person at a time; but that person may be the original father, or, after his death, the father's younger brother, whoever in the first ascending generation has succeeded to the office of father and taken over the rights and obligations of fatherhood in relation to ego. Similarly, with the term for "mother."

> As long as ego's real mother is alive and married to the man ego refers to as father, she alone is referred to as mother, and she alone plays the role of mother toward ego. If, through divorce or death, ego's real mother is no longer married to ego's father, and if he has not remarried, ego's real mother continues to be referred to as mother. If ego's father has remarried, the new wife is referred to as mother, she plays the role of mother toward ego, and ego may not refer to the divorced or dead woman as mother. (1953:231.)

With the levirate, likewise, if a man succeeds his brother as the holder of proprietary rights in his brother's wife—is his brother's heir to these rights—he may change the relationship term by which he refers to her when his brother's death changes the jural relationship in which he stands to her (now referring to her as "wife" rather than as "sister-in-law"). In the same vein, a man may refer to his father's sister's children by one term while his father lives, then by the term his father used for them after his father dies. My colleague Robert Netting tells me that such is the case among the Kofyar in Nigeria. Here a man has certain rights and duties relating to his sister's children. When he dies, his son apparently succeeds him as the holder of these rights and duties.

There are, then, societies in which the entitlements that go with particular kin relationships are nontransferable, and there are other societies in which they are seen as transferable. Where the entitlements can be transferred or succeeded to, all those in the line of succession may be classed together as the same kind of kinsman, as seems to be the case with some Crow and Omaha terminologies.[15] Instead of this, however, the kinship term may be applied only as succession takes place, thus producing the phenomenon Murdock and Kroeber have called the criterion of decedence or condition of life.

The criterion of decedence is, in this respect, like other conditions that affect the initiation and termination of the use of kinship terms. A man who is no kinsman of mine becomes my brother-in-law when he marries my sister. He acquires certain entitlements in relation to me, and I in relation to him, when he contracts to marry my sister. He ceases to be my brother-in-law when he and my sister get divorced, and the man who subsequently marries my sister becomes by brother-in-law in his stead. Similarly, a Siriono man in Bolivia uses a term for his female cross-cousins, who are the women from among who he will take a wife (Holmberg 1950:51–56). But when he marries one of them, he now calls her "wife." A similar situation holds for the Lakalai. Among them, all ego's in-laws were his consanguines before he married and will become his consanguines again, should he get divorced. The terms he uses for them change accordingly. The same thinking applies when death is seen to terminate a relationship with a particular person and to open the way for someone else to succeed to the relationship.

I have not tried to investigate the matter, but I suspect that the use of kinship terms in Africa is frequently affected by this idea of succession to some form of entitlement, some set of rights and obligations. I have already had occasion to remark on how important such considerations of entitlement are for some African societies in connection with proprietary rights in women and chil-

15. Whereas Omaha terminologies class cross-cousins with senior relatives on the maternal side and with junior relatives on the paternal side, as in the Kalmuk case, Crow terminologies do just the opposite, classing cross-cousins on the maternal side with junior relatives and on the paternal side with senior relatives (Spier 1925:73–74; Murdock 1949:224). For types of Crow and Omaha terminologies, see the brilliant analysis by Lounsbury (1964b).

dren, and I have raised questions accordingly regarding the anthropological handling of marriage and descent groups in these societies. The same considerations may underlie the problems of kinship usage in which the genealogically same positions among tertiary and remoter relatives may sometimes be denoted by a purely descriptive term and at other times by the classificatory extension of a term used for an immediate kinsman. I may be mistaken in this, but it strikes me as a possibility that those who work with African cultures may find worth looking into.

GENEALOGICAL DISTANCE

Componential analysis reveals criteria for discriminating categories of kinsmen that fall entirely outside the nine criteria of Kroeber and Murdock. An obvious one is what we can call genealogical distance. Murdock used the idea in defining what he called "primary," "secondary," and "tertiary" relatives (1949:94–95), but did not include it among his criteria of classification.

Units of genealogical distance can be defined in various ways, as Fischer (1960) has observed. Different terminologies define them differently. Common to all that I have seen is the use of a parent-child link in the consanguineal chain (a single generation gap) as a unit of distance when reckoning lineally. If one uses only this method of counting, then siblings are two units of distance away just as grandparents are (Figure 8).

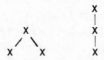

Figure 8. Siblings and grandparents as two parent-child links apart.

It is more common for kinship systems to count the sibling relationship (having a parent in common) as a unit of lateral distance, making siblings and parents equally one unit away. Murdock did this in defining his "primary" and "secondary" relatives. And this indeed is how it works in English terminology, as I know it, where, incidentally, a marital tie is not counted as a unit of distance, spouses being treated as alter-egos. Thus, at zero distance is ego, with *husband* and *wife* as the affinal alternates for that distance. At one degree of distance are *father, mother, brother, sister, son, daughter,* with the affinal alternates indicated by prefixing *step-* or suffixing *-in-law* to these terms. At two degrees of distance are *grandfather, grandmother, uncle, aunt, nephew, niece, grandson, granddaughter,* without specific affinal alternatives. Further degrees of distance within the range of two degrees of collateral removal are specified by using the adjective *great* (*grand* with *niece* and *nephew*) in front of the latter set of terms. One *great* specifies three degrees of distance, two of them specify four degrees of distance, and so on.[16]

With this mode of reckoning, kinsmen who are the same degree of distance from ego will be one generation apart in the lineal and first-degree collateral lines. *Grandfather* and *uncle,* for example, both designate second-degree relationships. For this reason we use one more *great* at the same generation level for the first-degree collaterals than we use for the lineal relatives in English terminology. This one generation discrepancy is a clear diagnostic indicator that degree of genealogical distance is a probable criterion of classification in a kinship system. The ancient Roman use of *nepos* for daughter's son and sister's son, and later for a child's son and sibling's son, is a possible example.[17]

The Kalmuk Mongols provide a well documented illustration of the use of this criterion (Aberle 1953, Adelman 1954). It applies to all *tör'l* who are younger in age or generation than ego. *Tör'l,* you will remember, are those kinsmen between whom and ego there are no female links. The distribution of these terms appears in Figure 9. Here the principle is that any degree of collateral distance counts as only one unit of genealogical distance. Terms 1 and 2 refer, therefore, to primary kinsmen (those at one degree of genealogical distance), term 3 denotes secondary kinsmen, term 4 denotes tertiary kinsmen, and so on. The criterion of genealogical

16. See my componential analysis of Yankee American terminology as I know it (1965a). A different approach is represented in Schneider's (1968a) important study of kinship in the Chicago area.
17. Floyd Lounsbury, to whom I am indebted for this example, interprets it differently.

distance accounts for this peculiar generation difference in usage for lineal and collateral relatives.

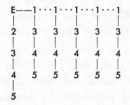

Figure 9. Distribution of Kalmuk Mongol kinship terms for relatives of tör'l type who are junior to ego. The solid horizontal line indicates a direct sibling link and the dotted lines more remote collateral connections. E = ego, 1 = düü, 2 = kövüün or küük'n, 3 = atche, 4 = dziiche, 5 = dziliike.

Genealogical distance can be construed as a criterion discriminating some kinds of affinal relationships among the Huichol of Mexico, but not in consanguineal relationships as Grimes and Grimes (1962) have claimed. Here a marital tie counts as a unit of distance (in contrast with English terminology). So, also, does each sibling link in lateral reckoning, and so does each parent-child link in lineal reckoning. A result is the interesting grouping under the same set of terms of the relationships diagrammed in Figure 10, both involving three degrees of genealogical distance.

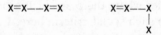

Figure 10. Huichol relationships classed together under the same terms. From Grimes and Grimes (1962).

STRUCTURAL EQUIVALENCE OR COINCIDENCE

Every conceivable relationship in genealogical space is distinct from every other. But rules of marriage and principles of social organization can work to create a tendency for certain relationships to coincide in the same persons. Anthropologists have long been interested in how such "coincidence," as Murdock (1949:136) called it, has served to bring distinct genealogical relationships together as the denotata of one kinship term, as when rules of marriage serve to make cross-cousin and spouse coincide.

Coincidence can also serve as a criterion for differentiating among the relationships denoted by kinship terms, in which role I have referred to it as "structural equivalence" (1964, 1965a). It seems to be especially important in connection with affinal relationships. Given marriage, the derivation of parenthood from it, an expectation of marital stability, and incest taboos, people will expect one's mother's husband to also be one's father and one's wife's child to also be one's own child. In common American usage, for example, the terms for primary consanguineal relationships are all prefixed by *step-* or suffixed by *-in-law* to denote relationships by marriage. All *step* relationships are structurally equivalent to (expected as a usual thing to coincide with) primary consanguineal ones, whereas no *in-law* relationships are. The criterion of structural equivalence accounts for the difference here. It accounts for a similar difference among the Könkämä Lapps (Goodenough 1964).

SOCIAL CRITERIA

Other criteria revealed by componential analysis take us into features of social organization of the kind I discussed in the second lecture. Membership in ego's patrilineal descent group as against membership in ego's mother's patrilineal descent group may be a criterion in societies where there are such groups, for example. But I shall not go into such social criteria here. I mention them only in order to emphasize that the criteria by which people classify their kin relationships are not necessarily confined to the properties of genealogical space or of positions within it.

CONCLUSION

In this excursion into the problems of kinship terminology, I have talked about such things as sex, age and temporal order, numerical counts, oddness and evenness, symmetry and asymmetry, similarity and difference (as of sex and generation) in relation to genealogical space. This space, whose possibilities for classifying kinsmen we have been exploring, is composed of parent-child links and marital ties. The comparative study of kinship terminology rests on the assumption that genealogical space is a cross-societal constant with reference to which kinship phenomena in all cultures can be defined, described, and compared. Yet this assumed constant is itself built out of marriage and parenthood.

When I discussed these two topics at length in Chapter I, I presented the problem of the search for universally applicable definitions as an exercise that would reveal some of the difficulties we face in description and comparison and left it at that. Now it becomes apparent why I regard it as more than just an interesting exercise.

We anthropologists have assumed that kinship is universal, that all societies have kinship systems. If we are correct in this assumption, if every human society does have some set of relationships whose definition involves genealogical considerations of some kind, then genealogical space must be constructed of things that are common to all mankind. These, we have seen, are parenthood and socially recognized sexual unions in which women are eligible to bear and from which women and especially men derive rights in children and thus establish parent-child relationships. If we cannot find a satisfactory way to conceptualize these things so that they withstand the test of cross-cultural application, we shall be unable to make meaningful comparison of the many ways in which people handle the classification of siblings and cousins.

4. General and Particular

In all I have said about marriage, parenthood, kin groups, and kinship terminology, I have been calling attention in passing to problems of description and comparison in cultural anthropology. I shall now speak to these problems directly.

Because I have chosen to talk of "cultural anthropology" in the title of these lectures rather than to talk of "social anthropology," I must clarify what I mean by culture as an object of study.

People who deal recurringly and frequently with one another develop expectations regarding the manner of conducting these dealings. They make some of their expectations explicit and formulate some of them as rules of conduct. They do not consciously formulate others but react to a person's failure to abide by them as a breach of appropriate behavior, saying that he behaves or talks oddly or in a mixed-up fashion. These expectations relate not only to social conduct but to how a person does his work, how he goes about accomplishing his purposes, and the beliefs and values he cites in justifying his own and others' acts.

The people who deal with one another and who have these expectations of one another do not necessarily agree on all the details of what they expect in their mutual dealings. But the variance in their individual expectations must be small enough so that they are able to accomplish their purposes with and through one another reasonably well most of the time. The variance between any two people of Truk or between any two country Irishmen regarding their expectations of fellow Trukese or fellow country Irish in speech and other forms of behavior, and in beliefs and values about most things, is considerably less than the variance between a man of Truk and an Irishman.

The expectations one has of one's fellows may be regarded as a set of standards for perceiving, believing, evaluating, communicating, and acting. These standards constitute the culture that one attributes to one's fellows; and it is in this sense of standards that I use the term culture here.[1] If operating according to the standards I attribute to the people of Truk results in behavior within the range of variance they accept as properly Trukese, then a description of those standards satisfactorily represents what we may call Trukese culture. It is a valid specimen of same. If acting according to my standards for country Irishmen results in behavior within the range of variance they accept as properly Irish, then my description of those standards satisfactorily represents what we may call country Irish culture.

In this respect a people's culture is like a people's language. For an account of a set of standards for speaking whose application results in speech within the variance Frenchmen accept as properly French is a satisfactory representation of the French language. If we wish to learn French, it is exactly what we want a grammar and dictionary of French to present.

No two persons in Truk have identical standards for what they regard as Trukese culture, and the amount of variance they accept in one another's behavior differs from one subject matter to another and from one kind of situation to another. For some subjects and situations, they are concerned to reduce the variance as much as possible and to achieve a sense of agreement as to what the standards are. They want no misunderstanding. In part, practical

---

1. I have elaborated on this view of culture elsewhere (1963:252–283; 1969). Similarly, Lévi-Strauss (1949:8) has observed, "Cette absence de règles semble apporter le critérium le plus sûr qui permette de distinguer un processus naturel d'un processus culturel."

considerations motivate such concern with reduction of variance. With language, for example, the more one desires to be understood by others and to understand them, the more one strives to use their speech behavior as a guide in constructing standards for one's own speech. Thus one minimizes the possibility of misunderstanding. Considerations of physical well-being motivate efforts to agree on standards, also, as in group acitivities in which failure to meet one another's expectations can easly result in death or injury. And, of course, emotional well-being motivates efforts to agree on standards. Where concern is high, the standards become explicitly formulated as precepts. In the conduct of social affairs—our concern in these lectures—the precepts define the rights and duties of various categories of person and group in relation to one another.

People have to work continually to maintain agreement (low variance) regarding standards, if for no other reason because of the continual dying off of older members of the community and the continual recruitment by birth of new members who do not have any knowledge of any standards at all. Seeking to learn to deal effectively with elders, on whom they depend for the accomplishment of their purposes, the young necessarily strive to develop for themselves standards of talking and behaving that will achieve the effects they desire. And the elders want the young to develop standards that bring their performance within the range of variance they are willing to accept. By precept and by reward and punishment they work to this end.

In any community, therefore, there are some people who are regarded as having greater knowledge of what the standards for the group are supposed to be. They are called upon to pronounce what the standards are in disputes about them. Thus, for some subjects at least, there are acknowledged authorities whose judgments regarding the agreed-upon standards and whose pronouncements as to whether something is right or wrong are accepted by others in the group. (Even the authorities do not always agree, of course.) People want such authorities.[2] Ethnographers con-

---

2. Consider, for example, the outrage expressed by many American reviewers of *Webster's Third New International Dictionary* because it reported the variance in popular usage without indicating what the editors, as presumed authorities, held to be "preferred" as distinct from "colloquial" usage within this variance (Sledd 1962).

cerned to describe a group's culture, in the sense in which I am using the term, make a regular practice of seeking out recognized local authorities and experts in order to use them as their principal sources of information, especially in matters of specialized knowledge and esoteric lore. Even in ordinary matters, one does not use a five-year-old as a reliable informant about adult activities. The authorities are, obviously, more likely to provide information from which an ethnographer can formulate for the community he studies a set of standards that, taken as a guide for acting and interpreting the acts of others, leads to behavior the community's members perceive as in accord with their expectations of one another—behavior they accept as being properly Trukese, country Irish, or whatever.

When I speak of describing a culture, then, formulating a set of standards that will meet this critical test is what I have in mind. There are many other things, too, that we anthropologists wish to know and try to describe. We have often referred to these other things as culture, also. Consequently, there are several senses of the term, and there is no general agreement among anthropologists as to what sense is the accepted one.[3] But that need not concern us here.

One matter does require comment, however. I have excluded from consideration in my definition of culture an account of the extent and nature of the variance in the standards that each member of a group individually attributes to his group. What the culture of a group is, I have said, is necessarily somewhat different for every one of the group's members.[4] If we already know how to get around in the United States as acceptably as most competently functioning Americans, what then interests us is the variance among Americans. But if we are immigrants from Japan, what interests us is getting a set of standards that allows us to operate competently. Accounts of variance confuse us and are largely irrelevant to the

3. The conflicting conceptions of culture among anthropologists have been reviewed by Kroeber and Kluckhohn (1952).
4. There are, of course, modalities within these differences. There is likely to be less variance among members of the same family than between members of different families. There will be less variance among members of the same work crew regarding the standards pertaining to its activities than between members of different work crews. These modalities represent what are often referred to as subcultures within a community or ethnic group.

problem we face. We want to know what we can accept as authoritatively "right," not the results of a survey of what a representative sample of Americans think is right. But the latter, of course, is precisely what we want if we wish to study the variance.

From one point of view, then, to describe a culture is to describe a set of standards whose behavioral manifestations local authorities will accept as appropriate. From another point of view, to describe a society's culture is to present an account of the individual variance in standards—much like the variance in the idiolects of the speakers of a language. The latter is, obviously, a much more complicated task than the former.

In practice, when anthropologists have described cultures with which they were unfamiliar, they have tended to concern themselves with what they understood to be authoritative. When they have dealt with variance, they have limited themselves to differences among specialists and laymen or among other subgroups and categories within a society. They have tended to disregard entirely individual cultural variance, although they have, of course, frequently concerned themselves with individual behavioral variance (which is something else, again). But when anthropologists take the same approach in relation to their own society, describing a set of standards that they, as competent persons, work with in their society, they are liable to be criticized for failure to consider the individual variance.[5] Some colleague is almost certain to say that with him it is different. Here is where we need to keep our signals straight.

5. Thus I have been criticized by Harris, who says (1968:586), "Goodenough has referred to his 'dialect' as a means of escaping the fact that *his* understanding of 'correct' kin terminological usage does not correspond to *mine*. Several important foci of functionally important ambiguity get swept under the rug by this maneuver." I would not deny that there are foci of ambiguity in the range of variance in American kinship usage. I agree that a description of my standards for using Yankee kinship terms obviously cannot provide the information needed to take account of such foci. In the article to which Harris refers, I was describing by componential analysis a particular pattern of American usage, not American patterns of usage (Goodenough 1965a). Harris misses the point that a Frenchman who uses my account as a guide for learning how to use English kinship terms in a Yankee manner will find that it will enable him to use them with Americans no more ambiguously than Americans use them with one another, and much less ambiguously when he deals with Americans whose pattern of usage is like my own.

In what I have to say here, I shall be speaking of a society's culture as a set of standards that seems to be authoritative. I shall not be concerned with culture as the total variance in the standards of a society's individual members, although I unreservedly accept the importance of such variance for cultural theory, not least as it pertains to problems in the theory of change.[6]

CULTURE AND SOCIAL STRUCTURE

A culture, as I am speaking of it, should not be confused with the things people habitually do nor with the prevailing arrangements and states of affairs that characterize a human society as a material-behavioral system of interacting people and things, exhibiting now greater and now less equilibrium in the course of time. The recurring or ongoing arrangements that characterize its equilibrium may be said to portray a society's structure; but they are not its culture. They are the products or artifacts of what people in that society have been doing in response to the situations confronting them, as they perceive and understand them.[7] What they have been doing has been guided by their purposes as they have defined them and also, presumably, by their unconscious motives. Their definitions of purpose, their perception of situations, and their responses to them have been in considerable part guided by the standards the individual members of the society attribute to their fellow members and perceive as the culture of their society. The recurring arrangements in a community are thus in part an indirect product of its members' culture; they are also in part a product of events and conditions over which people in the community have little or no control, all the way from floods and storms to their own animal natures.

Whatever the prevailing arrangements in a community are, however, what they are perceived to be depends very much on the culture of the beholder. Consider, for example, the different conclusions of John Fischer and myself some years ago about residential arrangements on Romónum Island in Truk (Good-

---

6. How such variance relates to problems of change has been of some theoretical interest to me (1961b, 1963).

7. In this I concur with Barth (1966), who sees structure as a resultant of the choices or decisions people make in transactions.

enough 1956b). We each took a house-by-house census, making a complete record of every married couple's domestic location, but our conclusions regarding the statistical pattern of arrangement differed. We could not agree on the kind of residence each Trukese couple was in, even though we were using the same set of anthropological terms on whose definition in the abstract we agreed quite well. The cause of our difference was our different conceptions of the objects of residential choice as the Trukese perceived them. Our different cultures for Truk led to different pictures of the prevailing social structure. To start with the objects of choice as the Trukese perceive them, as they are defined by the standards of Trukese culture, results in a different structure from one arrived at by projecting on them an erroneous conception of their culture, the categories of one's own folk culture, or the categories of one's own professional anthropological culture.

Many problems in anthropology require the use of concepts that are not a part of the culture of the people under study, as Ford (1966) has reminded us. But problems such as the one with which Fischer and I were concerned do require us to know the concepts with which they work, insofar as it is possible to know them. Whenever we wish to know what people are doing and why, or what they are likely to do, we must know what phenomena they see, for these are the phenomena to which they respond. And we must know what they believe to be the relations among these phenomena and what they perceive as the possible courses of action for dealing with them. Such knowledge is crucial to an understanding of their jural ordering of social relations, including the things I have been discussing in these lectures.

DESCRIBING A CULTURE

A major problem for anthropology, then, is how to describe other people's cultures—their standards for perceiving, believing, evaluating, and acting.

The problem is not unlike describing a game, a very complicated one. There are the different categories of person, which correspond to the different pieces on the board or the several positions on the team. There are the different categories of object, both natural and manufactured, which bound and define the universe or playing field of the game. Within the restrictions imposed by these bounds and by the physical constitution of the players, there are additional restrictions on the moves that any one category of person can make in relation to each category of object and each other category of person. These restrictions are the rules of the game. The game has its agreed-upon objectives: wealth, honor, many attentive grandchildren, power, whatever it is that is publicly accepted as indicative of personal fulfillment, success, or the good life. The game is complicated, moreover, in that there are many lesser games within it, some of which are required for all participants and others of which are optional.

I need not go on filling out the analogy. It has been drawn before. Indeed, a game is nothing but a miniature and highly formalized culture.[8]

The point of the analogy is this. Suppose you have come to the United States from England with the object of describing the game of American football to your fellow Englishmen. To describe it in the language of rugby is not going to be altogether satisfactory—even though the two games are related. To describe it in the language of military maneuver and physical combat will also be somewhat misleading. In either case, the English reading audience would get some rough idea of American football, but at best it would be a caricature of the game as Americans know it. We are all familiar with such caricatures. The problem of ethnography is how to describe the culture of another people for an audience that is unfamiliar with it so that the description is not a caricature but presents a set of standards that satisfactorily represent what one needs to know to play the game acceptably by the standards of those who already know how to play it—or if not to play it, to understand it as well as those who know how to play it understand it and in terms that permit discussing it knowledgeably with them.

As I said in the first chapter, I conceive of the problem as no different, in principle, from the one we face when we describe a language (see also Burling 1969). There is a stream of sound

8. On games and culture, see especially Atkins and Curtis (1968), and Buchler and Selby (1968:100–102). Roberts and Sutton-Smith (1962) have developed the idea that games are models of features of adult culture by which people rehearse roles they play in life. They also suggest how different kinds of games are related to the different kinds of emotional demands that various life-roles make.

emanating from the speaker's mouth. An uninitiated hearer can perceive the sound in many different ways. To describe what we need to know in order to speak and hear the language correctly, as judged by its native speakers, a linguist must tell us how we are to perceive the stream of sound. If he tries to describe it in terms of the sound categories of English, as represented by the English alphabet, or by the grammatical categories of Latin, as some early linguists tried to do, the result will be a caricature.[9]

To avoid this result, a linguist begins his account by defining the minimum number of behavioral units that a speaker must learn to discriminate. These include modalities of sound that have stimulus value for the language's speakers. These elementary sound units with stimulus value serve to discriminate one linguistic act for what it is from other linguistic acts. Thus we hear a difference between the words we spell as *night* and *light*. The people of Truk have difficulty hearing this difference, because the sound modes we write with *n* and *l* overlap with parts of one sound mode in their language. Native speakers of English have similar difficulty learning the elementary sound modes of other languages. Analysis of what makes the difference among these sound modes as distinct stimuli results in a set of "distinctive features," the modal values of phonetic variables.

The distinctive features, the ultimate irreducible units of a language, in their various combinations make up the modal units of sound, the phonemes. The phonemes are ordered into more complex units, each of which conveys some specific kind of meaning. And these more complex units are ordered, in turn, into still more complex units, such as phrases, sentences, and narratives. A description of each of these more complex levels of organization is a statement of how the units of less complex levels may be acceptably juxtaposed and combined. At these higher levels, all descriptive statements are about the order among elements that are themselves a part of the language being described. They are not elements of

9. In the language of Truk, for example, it is necessary to distinguish nine short vowels (Dyen 1949), which partly overlap and cut across the vowel distinctions of English. The five vowel symbols of the English alphabet do not satisfactorily represent the vowels of English; they were designed for Latin. They are even less satisfactory for the vowel phonemes of Trukese.

some other language. Thus we build up our account of a language in terms of its own primitive elements and the units constructed out of them.[10]

But we cannot describe the primitive elements in terms of themselves. To describe these, we need some independent perceptual and conceptual frame, one that a linguist brings with him into the descriptive task and that is part of a culture and is represented symbolically in a language he already knows and shares with the audience to whom he presents his description. If the culture and language of description—the metaculture and metalanguage—are too crude conceptually and symbolically to provide a definition of the primitive elements in the language to be described, it is inadequate for description; what will result will be a distorted caricature of the kind I referred to above. It would be as if a linguist from Truk used the elementary sounds of the Trukese language to describe the elementary sounds of English and treated *light* and *night, sully* and *sunny, yawl* and *yawn* as if there were no perceptible difference in each of these pairs. Or it would be as if an English account of Trukese treated *kkón* ("breadfruit pudding") and *kkóón* ("lying down") or *mwáán* ("man") and *mmwáán* ("wrong") as if they were identical in form, failing to take account of the significant distinction in Trukese between long and short vowels and long and short consonants.

To describe languages satisfactorily, linguists had to learn to make new discriminations of sound, ones they had not been familiar with before. They then had to find some way of describing and symbolizing these new sound discriminations. As they continued to encounter more and more new discriminations and added them to the growing list of what served as distinctive features in different languages, they began to find it possible to systematize what they had been discovering and to isolate the various parameters of sound production, such as position of articulation, aspiration, voicing,

10. It does not follow that the procedures by which a linguist isolates the various kinds of unit at each level of complexity are similarly ordered, starting with lower levels before proceeding to more complex ones. The choice among alternative analyses of lower levels may be determined by what one learns about the way things are ordered at higher levels. For a résumé of linguistic procedures, see Lounsbury (1953). For an example of their application to ethnography, see Burling (1969).

nasalization, lateralization, spirantization, etc. Out of this emerged a kit of concepts and symbols with which the phonemes and distinctive features of any language could be described (e.g., Bloch and Trager 1942, Pike 1943). This same kit provided the constants by which the phonemes and distinctive features of different languages could be compared and by which changes in a language's phonemes or ordering of distinctive features could be described (Hoenigswald 1960).

Linguists refer to the task of isolating and describing the sound modalities of particular languages as "phonemics," and they refer to the study of sound production and the development of a metalanguage by which the phonemes and distinctive features of any language can be described as "phonetics." Both kinds of operation are essential to linguistic science, and neither is possible without the other. For by trying to learn what the phonemes of a particular language are, we learn new sound discriminations that we did not know existed before. We then add these new discriminations to the phonetic kit of possibilities with which we approach the task of describing the next language. Systematizing the contents of the phonetic kit allows for controlled comparison and provides the foundation of a general theory of speech sounds consistent with the phenomena of all languages, with all their differences.

The same can be said for the problem of describing the grammatical categories and principles of syntax of different languages. As we learn new principles of syntactic order, we add to the kit of possibilities. The more languages we study, the less we find it necessary to add to the kit. Systematization of its contents, of the many different principles of syntactic order we have encountered in specific languages, lays the foundations for a general theory of syntax.

But what is a language if not a set of standards for human conduct of a particular kind?[11] Description and comparison of standards of human conduct of any kind must involve similar considerations. This thought in mind, Pike (1967) has generalized from phonetics and phonemics to what he has called the "etics" and "emics" of all socially meaningful human behavior. Whatever the names one may choose to call them, these concepts of the etic and

11. Anthropologists are increasingly recognizing that language is indeed an aspect or part of culture, as Casagrande (1963:220) has observed.

the emic are indispensable for understanding the problems of description and comparison, of the particular and the general, in cultural anthropology.

I can illustrate from my own ethnographic work on Truk. When I tried to prepare an account of the workings of Truk's social organization (1951), I found that I could not satisfactorily describe kinship terminology without having first described kin-group organization. Membership in kin groups was one of the considerations that made sense of the way Truk's people classified kin relationships. And I could not describe kin-group organization without having first described how property worked. The most important kind of kin group was a property-holding corporation. So my description began with the several property transactions and the resulting forms of entitlement that Truk's rules of the social game allowed. Definition of the descent groups could then be made in terms of these forms of entitlement, and so on. Thus I tried to build up an account of the culture of social organization in Truk from a set of what seemed to me to be elementary or primitive concepts in Trukese culture.

The combinations of rights that characterize Trukese forms of entitlement are not precisely like those with which an English-speaking audience is familiar. Such English expressions as "fee simple," "sale," "loan," "rental," and "ownership" could not serve in their English senses as useful terms for describing property in Truk. To be satisfactory, my account had to exhaust the forms of entitlement and the kinds of transaction that were meaningfully distinct for the people of Truk; and the labels I used for them in my description had to be defined in terms of whatever criteria enabled me to distinguish among the entitlements and transactions in a manner consistent with the distinctions the people of Truk seemed to be making.

Once the emic primitives were isolated and satisfactorily defined, I could then proceed to an account of how they combined to make more complex social forms and how these forms, in turn, combined to make even more complex social and political groupings. This approach is what anthropologists have in mind—those who use the phrase—when they say it is necessary to describe a culture "in its own terms." They do not mean that one must describe the primitive elements tautologically in terms of themselves. They mean that having isolated and defined the primitive elements, one goes on to describe the rest of the culture in terms of them and their relative products. Thus one takes one's audience into the culture of another people and allows it to experience that culture and to learn something of it from the insider's (the sophisticate's) point of view.

To describe the forms of transaction and entitlement that were the primitive elements in the Truk case, as I have said, I had to make conceptual distinctions that were new to me. Trukese distinctions do not cut the pie of property as Anglo-American distinctions do. The concepts I developed for Truk proved helpful to Oliver (1955) in conceptualizing and describing the culture of property relations among the Siuai of Bougainville. The notions of "divided ownership," "residual title," and "provisional title" were now a part of the etic kit of possibilities available to Oliver for describing how things worked among the Siuai. As others continue to meet new ways of discriminating among transactions and forms of entitlement in other cultures, they will continue to add to our knowledge of possibilities. In time, we shall be able to give order to the ideas we have had to develop to describe the elementary emic forms in a large sample of the world's cultures. In ordering these ideas, we shall isolate the considerations with which human beings tend to organize their property relations and shall lay the foundations for a general theory of property that will account for the variance among cultures in the way they employ these considerations. Such theory, it is now clear, depends on the development of a satisfactory etics of property relations, and this latter development depends on our doing many good emic descriptions of particular property systems.

So a science of culture rests on description. We have known this all along, to be sure. But we have tended to think of description as simply a matter of presenting the "objective" facts about a society, its organization, law, customs, and shared beliefs in terms of the audience's culture and the audience's interests, as if that culture and those interests were all that are involved in depicting the objective facts about people who have different cultures and different interests. We have not been seriously concerned to understand what one has to know to behave acceptably as a member of an Australian aboriginal tribe any more than zoologists have been seriously concerned, until very recently, to know how to behave acceptably as an ostrich.[12] We wanted to know *about* other societies, not how to be competent in the things their members are expected to be competent in. Our best ethnographies were, to be sure, coming from people whose interests and circumstances led them to want to know how to operate successfully with people in other societies on their terms or, at least, to communicate with them competently about their activities and beliefs in their language, whether they were anthropologists (e.g., Malinowski 1922, 1935; Firth 1936), missionaries (e.g., Junod 1927), or government administrators (e.g., Rattray 1929). But none thought of himself as writing a "how-to-do-it" book. The closest thing to this has been provided by a few accounts of technology or arts and crafts (e.g., Buck 1930, 1944).

I do not think that how-to-do-it books are what all ethnographic accounts should aim to be. Far from it! But by failing to see such an orientation as appropriate to the task of ethnography, fundamentally appropriate, we have tended until recently to neglect the emics of ethnography. And to the extent that we have neglected the emics, we have failed to develop a satisfactory etics. Technology illustrates the point. Here etic concepts are much more highly developed precisely because technology has a long tradition of instruction in how to do it.

It should now be clear why I have been interested in problems of ethnographic description from an emic viewpoint in my own work. It should also be clear why I consider the interest some anthropologists have taken in these matters in the past fifteen years under the somewhat misleading headings of "ethnoscience" and "the new ethnography" to be a constructive development.[13] Experi-

12. The work in recent decades in animal behavior known as ethology represents, of course, a significant change in this attitude by zoologists and primatologists.

13. For reviews see Sturtevant (1964) and Goodenough (1969). Because the emphasis in much of this kind of ethnographic work has been on descriptive semantics, a further comment is in order. To speak a language competently obviously requires developing standards for using its vocabulary in a way that will seem "correct" to native speakers. To learn the meaning

ence tells us that how other people construe things is one of the major concerns of every human being from early childhood on. By arriving at empirically workable conclusions about just this, a growing child makes himself acceptable to his fellows and able to accomplish his purposes in his dealings with them. What nearly every human being manages to do with a reasonable degree of success is clearly a proper object of scientific study. To understand the process involved is fundamental to an understanding of how culture can be said to be *shared* by a society's members or how "collective representations," to use Durkheim's phrase for it, can be said to be *collective*. When we speak of the emic aspect of ethnography, we are concerned with precisely this problem in that we want to know how an ethnographer can come to share a set of understandings with the people he studies and how he can in turn share these same understandings with the audience for whom he writes an ethnographic report.

In a major work Harris (1968:568–604) has expressed his fear that concern with emics is becoming too fashionable and that an etic approach of the kind he has outlined in another work (1964), which he regards as more in keeping with the aims and spirit of science, will be neglected. As I have said, emic description requires etics, and by trying to do emic descriptions we add to our etic conceptual resources for subsequent description. It is through etic concepts that we do comparison. And by systematizing our etic concepts we contribute to the development of a general science of culture.[14] Therefore, I agree heartily with Harris about the fundamental importance of etics. But unlike him I see etics as bogging down in useless hairsplitting and overpreoccupation with recording hardware, unless it is accompanied by a concern for emics. For Harris, concern with emic description competes with the development of etics; for me, it contributes most directly to it.

---

of words is, thus, to acquire an apparent understanding of the concepts of the people who use those words. Descriptive semantics is therefore an important approach contributing to the emic description of cultures. But people have concepts that are not represented by the vocabulary of their languages. Emic description requires methods in addition to those of descriptive semantics, as illustrated by the work of Berlin, Breedlove, and Raven (1968).

14. Buchler and Selby (1968) also repeatedly emphasize that attention to good description (emics) will produce better bases of comparison (etics).

ETICS AND TYPOLOGY

We come back now to what I have been talking about in the preceding chapters. All of it has had to do with problems of an etic
nature. This is clearest, perhaps, in the third chapter, where I discussed the criteria for differentiating and classifying kinds of kin
relationships.

It has been obvious to anthropologists that one cannot equate
such things as Trukese *semey* and English *father,* except in the
sense that both of the designated categories include ego's jural male
parent. Beyond this, the specific relationships that *semey* and
father may denote are different. (And this difference does not begin
to take account of the differences in jural obligation that attend
these categories in Truk and the United States.) To compare kinship terminologies, we are forced back to the criteria employed in
classifying relatives or to statements about the sets of kin types the
various terms designate. Thus we see one terminology making a
lineal-collateral distinction and another one not. Two other terminologies both make distinctions according to sex differences among
coeval pairs in the genealogical chain but in different ways.

So bit by bit, as better description and better analysis of data
already recorded have forced us to refine our etic concepts, we
have increased our potential for systematic comparison. I cited
Kroeber's (1909) work as a major step in this direction,[15] and I

15. Harris (1968:577) has accused Sturtevant (1964) of making the
"historically misleading claim that Kroeber's 1909 treatment of the semantic
dimensions of kinship was 'the basic paper on the etics of kinship.' But . . .
the whole point of Kroeber's famous article was to replace Morgan's sociological treatment of kinship with a linguistic treatment." Indeed, Kroeber was
saying that kinship terminology must be understood from the point of view
of psychology (or what we would now call cognition) rather than of
sociology. (See especially the comments on this by Schneider 1968.) But
Harris misunderstands the role of etics in ethnography and general anthropology and its relation to emics. For him (1968:575), "An ethnography
carried out according to etic principles is thus a corpus of predictions about
the behavior of classes of people. Predictive failures in that corpus require
reformulation of the probabilities or the description as a whole." Apparently,
he does not see that reformulations of one's concepts to bring one's description into better accord with predictions regarding certain kinds of informant
reactions are what lead to emic ethnography. What Harris seems to mean by
etics is evidently not what Pike (1967), who coined the term, I, or others he

then went on to show how componential analysis is requiring us to make further refinements in our etic kit and is laying the basis for an even more systematic account of how the properties of genealogical space can be employed in their various combinations to describe the emic categories of kin relationships.[16]

How such refinement of the etics of kinship has improved our capability for controlled comparison is clear in the historical record. Because kinship terminologies were not emicly described in the early days of investigation by Morgan (1871)—though often his data were very full—the typology of differences in kinship systems was inevitably crude, as illustrated by Morgan's "classificatory" and "descriptive" types. One could report lots of data, but what one could say about them was limited. Kroeber's analysis of existing data and identification of eight criteria, albeit for purposes other than dealing with problems of description and comparison, marked an important advance. Thereafter, anthropologists frequently used his criteria in describing and comparing kinship terminologies, and Lowie (1929) used two of them to construct a new typology of kinship systems.[17]

---

criticizes mean by it. Harris has failed to learn the "culture" of those he criticizes. He commits the old mistake, which all of us have made, of equating the emic categories of another culture directly with the different emic categories of his own. The caricature he thus makes of the other culture is what he proceeds to find fault with. Thus, what is in some ways a brilliant and provocative work suffers in its treatment of "etics and emics" from having the subject out of focus so that its polemics are aimed at a strawman. Kroeber's stated purposes for examining the criteria of kinship classification are, of course, irrelevant to Sturtevant's thoroughly appropriate statement.

16. That my work with componential analysis has dealt with the problem of describing emic categories of culture as these categories are reflected by the linguistic labels people use for them does not mean that I regard semantic analysis as the only means of getting at emic categories, even of kinship categories. Nor do I regard it as in itself a sufficient means for getting at all the emic categories of a culture. Linguistic labels are only one kind of behavioral form whose elements are differentially distributed in relation to other emic elements of a culture. The method of finding where something makes a difference for one's informants can be carried on with respect to the way in which any set of behaviors or phenomena distribute with respect to any other set of behaviors or phenomena. See Berlin, Breedlove, and Raven (1968), Burling (1969), and Keesing (1970b).

17. Murdock (1949:141–142) gives a detailed exposition of the typology and of the various groupings of kin types under each type within it.

Confining his attention to parents, children, parents' true siblings, and true siblings' children, Lowie saw all possible groupings and distinctions in one generation among them as products of how the criteria of lineality-collaterality and bifurcation (sex of the linking relative)[18] were employed in conjunction with one another. Thus he produced the four types shown in Figure 11 and illustrated on a genealogical diagram in Figure 12.

Type of kin nomenclature	Lineal distinguished from collateral	Distinction based on bifurcation
Bifurcate collateral	Yes	Yes
Bifurcate merging	No	Yes
Lineal	Yes	No
Generation	No	No

Figure 11. Types of kin nomenclature, after Lowie (1929).

Meanwhile, Spier (1925) had developed another classification of kinship terminologies based on the ways in which first cousins were grouped or distinguished from siblings, aunts and uncles, nephews and nieces, and one another, as revealed empirically by a comparative study of kinship terminology in North American Indian cultures. His typology was subsequently reworked by Murdock (1949:223–224; 1967:158). It is based on the way specific kintypes equate with other specific kintypes within a limited corpus of the total range of kintypes covered by kinship terms,[19] as was

18. Actually, it is not the sex of the linking relative but the presence of a sex difference between the parent of the junior relative and the senior party to the relationship (the coeval pair) that accounts for what is called bifurcation here, as is evident in Figure 12.

19. As given by Murdock (1967:158), with some rearrangement of order, the typology is (1) *Descriptive,* with "descriptive or derivative, rather than elementary, terms employed for all cousins"; (2) *Crow,* with "FaSiCh equated with Fa or FaSi and/or MoBrCh with Ch or BrCh(ws)"; (3) *Omaha,* with "MoBrCh equated with MoBr or Mo and/or FaSiCh with SiCh(ms) or Ch"; (4) *Sudanese,* with "FaSiCh and MoBrCh distinguished alike from siblings, parallel cousins, and each other but without conforming to either the Crow, the descriptive, or the Omaha patterns"; (5) *Iroquois,* with "FaSiCh equated with MoBrCh but differentiated from both siblings and parallel cousins"; (6) *Eskimo,* with "FaBrCh, FaSiCh, MoBrCh, and

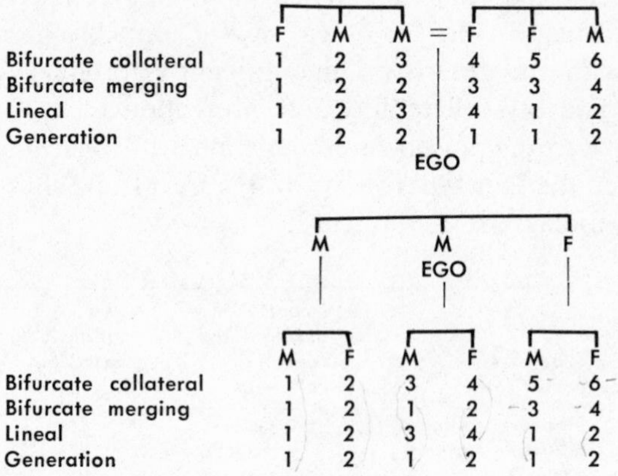

	F	M	M	=	F	F	M
Bifurcate collateral	1	2	3		4	5	6
Bifurcate merging	1	2	2		3	3	4
Lineal	1	2	3		4	1	2
Generation	1	2	2		1	1	2

EGO

M   M   F
EGO

	M	F	M	F	M	F
Bifurcate collateral	1	2	3	4	5	6
Bifurcate merging	1	2	1	2	3	4
Lineal	1	2	3	4	1	2
Generation	1	2	1	2	1	2

Note: numbers represent kinship terms; M = male; F = female. The examples shown assume that sex of alter is also distinguished; but this distinction is irrelevant for the typology.

Figure 12. Diagram of Lowie's types of kin nomenclature.

also the case with Lowie's typology; but it does not try to express these equations systematically in terms of Kroeber's or any other criteria of kinship.[20]

Systematization by rules for expansion from or reduction to the nearest kintype (to ego) denoted by a term has since been undertaken by Lounsbury (1964b) in an elegant refinement of Spier's and Murdock's Crow and Omaha types. His approach (transformational analysis) is readily extended to a systematic handling of any kinship terminology (Buchler and Selby 1968) and represents a

---

MoSiCh equated with each other but differentiated from siblings"; (7) *Hawaiian*, with "all cousins equated with siblings or called by terms clearly derivative from those for siblings"; (8) *Mixed*, with "mixed or variant patterns not adequately represented by any of the foregoing."

20. Kirchhoff (1932) developed a typology almost identical with Lowie's in which he also included analogous groupings of kin types for siblings and first cousins. His types correspond to Lowie's and Murdock's types as follows: *Type A* = Bifurcate collateral plus Sudanese or Descriptive types; *Type B* = Lineal plus Eskimo types; *Type C* = Generation plus Hawaiian types; *Type D* = Bifurcate merging plus Iroquois types.

major development in the etics of kinship study, providing an important alternative to the method of componential analysis. But its application still requires emic definitions of parenthood in order to establish what are kintypes and genealogical connections in each culture under analysis.

Inevitably, a question arises whether developments in the etics of kinship, progressively adding to the variables (criteria) and operations on them from which emic categories can be satisfactorily described, do not invalidate or render suspect, at least, the propositions about kinship terminology based on older typologies.

For example, many kinship systems have been regarded as "lineal" and "Eskimo" in type because they classed all parents' siblings together as distinct from parents and all first cousins together as distinct from siblings. They were so typed without regard to how the kin terms involved distributed over the total corpus of kintypes to which kin terms could refer. Thus the Kalingas of the Philippines class all relatives in the parents' generation with the parents' siblings (Barton 1949:68–69), whereas traditional usage among northeastern Americans is to class all consanguineal relatives in the parents' generation other than parents' siblings as *cousins* along with relatives other than siblings in ego's generation. A componential analysis shows American kinship categories to be stratified vertically into a set of relatives who are two or more degrees of collateral distance from ego (all categorized as *cousins*), as distinct from a more immediate set of relatives who are less than two degrees of collateral distance and who are differentiated by the great bulk of American terms according to genealogical distance from ego. Among the Kalingas, on the other hand, the fundamental stratification is a horizontal one, based on degree of generation removal. At two or more degrees of distance, all kintypes are classed together; at one degree of distance, lineal are distinguished from all degrees of collateral kin, which are lumped together; and in ego's generation, distinctions are made according to each degree of collateral distance, with siblings, and first, second, and third cousins all categorized separately. The semantic and conceptual structures of the two terminologies are radically different. The only overlap is in the use of collateral distinctions of some kind, but even these distinctions are not used in the same way. It is an artifact of the different cultural principles of each system that the particular kintypes with reference to which the lineal and Eskimo types of nomenclature were formulated are grouped in the same way in both. What then do we make of the lineal and Eskimo types and the typologies they represent?

With this question we confront the role of typology in scientific inquiry and, with it, basic issues in comparative study and in the general science of man and culture. To set the stage for a discussion of these issues, I shall briefly examine the use Murdock (1949) made of these typologies to test a general postulate about the "determinants of kinship terminology."

He considered these determinants to be the associations and disassociations of kintypes resulting from the ways kinsmen are brought together and separated from one another under the various forms of family organization, domestic group, descent group, and the like. From his postulate he deduced a series of theorems, which he examined statistically against a sample of the world's societies. I shall illustrate with his Theorem 14 (1949:157): "In the absence of clans and of polygamous and extended families, the isolated nuclear family tends to be associated with kinship terminology of the lineal type."

Murdock's use of Lowie's and Spier's typologies in this manner to test his postulate presupposes that the determinants he is considering exert the greatest influence on the grouping of kintypes genealogically nearest to ego with the kintypes next most close. That the Kalingas and Yankees lack descent groups, practice monogamy, and prefer to have each married couple in a separate household serves in both cases, according to the postulate, to make social relations between primary kinsmen markedly different from relations between more distant kinsmen, who are usually in different households. The Kalingas and Yankees may group the remoter kintypes in different ways, but that is not relevant for examining the effect of isolated nuclear families on the classification of kinsmen. Thus it may be an artifact of the two cultural systems that near kintypes are categorized in conformity with Lowie's lineal type. But the type of artifact may be one that people with fundamentally different cultures tend to create when they are subjected to similar constraints in their social environments. Having different cultural resources to begin with, they achieve these similar artifacts by different cultural means, just as clay pots suitable for boiling food can be made by peoples with different ceramic traditions using different techniques. Although Kalinga and Yankee kinship terminologies are culturally distinct, they are in some ways functionally analogous.

Thus viewed, resort to the lineal type in this particular theorem seems appropriate to the assumptions on which Murdock based his postulate. Other postulates involving other considerations will necessarily require the invention of new classifications appropriate to the questions asked. We must agree with Leach (1961) and Scheffler (1966) that nothing is sacrosanct about any typology, established or otherwise. It is simply useful for certain purposes. And its relation to the purposes for which it is to be used must always be carefully examined.

COMPARATIVE STUDY

The foregoing example gives us a glimpse of basic problems and issues in comparative study. I shall approach them with reference to our purposes in making comparison. These, we have seen, are directly relevant to how we categorize the things we would compare—to how we select or construct suitable typologies. If we think of our methods and typologies as means to ends, knowledge of our ends provides a basis for judging the suitability of the tools we have devised for achieving them.

The simplest and most direct kind of comparison is to look at two different cultures with the object of seeing in what ways they are similar or different in content. Do the standards of culture *A* governing the relations between spouses resemble those of culture *B*? How do they compare with respect to the ordering of property relationships? With respect to their cosmologies?

As I have said, such comparison requires some set of common terms suitable for describing the content of each culture—a set of etic concepts, such as the various criteria of kinship described in chapter 3. But it requires something else as well: some basis for deciding what set of forms in culture *A* are the appropriate ones to compare with a particular set of forms in culture *B*.

Many different bases are possible, and what one we choose depends on the purpose of our comparison. One, however, is so common that we tend to take it for granted as a natural basis for comparison. It has produced a typology of cultural forms comprising the standard vocabulary with which we ordinarily talk about cultures and thus implicitly, if not explicitly, compare them. This vocabulary includes such terms as "property," "marriage," "kinship," "religion," "political organization," "warfare"—virtually the entire list of things Murdock (1945) once gave as representing what he called the "common denominator" of cultures.[21]

But when we compare property relationships in two cultures, by what criteria do we decide that we are dealing with something we can call "property" in each case? Or "marriage," "kinship," "religion," etc.? Clearly they do not pertain to the content of cultural forms but to the roles these forms seem to play in people's lives— to the conscious and unconscious ends for which people seem to use them (or to try to use them) as means, and to the kinds of outputs that seem to result from their use in the conduct of affairs. These terms, in short, reflect functional considerations. We label "property" in Truk the cultural forms that seem to be the functional analogues of what we already label "property" in Anglo-American culture. So, too, with "marriage," as we had occasion to consider in the first chapter.

Functional classifications enter implicitly, if not explicitly, into almost all the comparisons of culture that anthropologists have made.[22] They have provided the one set of presumed universals or common denominators of culture, taking for granted that all people everywhere have similar problems and concerns arising from their common humanity. For this reason, my search for a universally

21. See also the shorter list of categories in Wissler's (1923) "universal culture pattern," and the later discussion of "universal categories of culture" by Kluckhohn, who said (1953:520), "there is a generalized framework that underlies the more apparent and striking facts of cultural relativity. All cultures constitute so many somewhat distinct answers to essentially the same questions posed by human biology and by the generalities of the human situation."

22. The importance of functional considerations in comparative linguistics stands out clearly in a recent symposium on the universals of language (Greenberg 1963).

applicable definition of marriage in the first lecture was not a meaningless exercise.

Aside from the direct comparison of two or more cultures with
reference to similarity and difference in their content, most comparison in anthropology has been with an eye to testing or exploring
a proposition. We may consider the propositions that have provided
the purposes of comparison under three general headings.

First, there are propositions about the interrelations of cultural
forms. To examine these we need a typology of the forms that is
relevant to the proposition. The following proposition provides an
example: Kinship terminologies in which generation distinctions
are the basic (or among the basic) criteria will be more likely to
use the presence of sex differences among siblings and/or coeval
pairs in the genealogical chain as additional criteria than will kinship terminologies in which generation distinctions are a minor
consideration relative to either collaterality or genealogical distance.[23]

The typology of forms appropriate to such a proposition involves
the relevance or irrelevance of particular etic criteria of kinship for
describing the emic categories in the cultures compared. But the
identification of the terminologies as kinship terminologies takes us
back to a cross-cultural definition of kinship, which, we have seen,
derives in turn from a cross-cultural definition of parenthood. And
definition of the latter, we saw, rested on certain facts of human
nature that are a matter of universal concern. For this reason I
could define parenthood as the cultural forms (whatever their
shape) by which people handle a common concern relating to these
facts. At base the definition was a functional one. So, too, was my
definition of marriage. These definitions also included reference to
jural rights, but the definition of rights rests, in turn, on concerns
that are common to all people and is also functionally based, as I
have had occasion to indicate elsewhere (1963:65, 95–97).

The emic entities in different cultures (and languages) that we
equate with reference to an appropriate set of etic concepts, we
are compelled to recognize, are so equated by virtue of some kind

23. I think this proposition is valid, but the comparative data needed to
verify or falsify it have yet to be assembled.

of function. The phonemes of a language are the several different combinations of distinctive features of sound that function to distinguish one verbal stimulus from another. Phonetics pertains to the description and analysis of the features of sound that function in this way. As a part of the etics of kin relationships, the criteria discussed in the third chapter are the ones by which people distinguish among the categories within a larger class of relationships whose definition as a class rests ultimately on functional considerations. Thus the very things for which we seek to develop etic concepts are categories of subject matter that have been functionally derived.

I see nothing wrong with this. Most human behavior is purpose-oriented. We are acutely uncomfortable when we are driven by an inner unease or tension that we cannot translate into purpose and thereby focus our behavior with reference to it. I have devoted the major part of a book (1963) to what human purposefulness and willfulness imply for understanding the various functional analogies between cultural forms and for understanding also the processes by which cultural forms and social institutions are developed, maintained, and changed. The fundamentally functional orientation of anthropological science is appropriate to its subject matter and to its practitioners alike. But we must not forget what our orientation is or neglect its implications for theory and method just because it comes naturally to us.

Although propositions about the interrelations of cultural forms involve implicit, underlying considerations of function, they are not in themselves propositions about the functions of cultural forms. They pertain to the internal structuring of the content of culture. By contrast, propositions of the second kind, to which I now turn, are about the relations of cultural forms to extra-cultural phenomena, such as prevailing conditions in society (including its equilibrium), prevailing emotions and moods, the general level of health, or the condition of the physical environment. They are propositions about the place of cultural forms in a larger ecological setting.

These propositions take two principal forms. One has to do with the effect of prevailing extra-cultural conditions on the form of cultural standards and rules. It deals with the "causes" of cultural forms. An example is Murdock's (1949:201ff) thesis that a statistically prevalent alignment of kin in domestic units (as a result of residence decisions) will tend to produce a cultural principle of membership in descent groups that is consistent with that alignment (should occasion arise for the development of descent groups in addition to domestic groups). The antecedent or independent variable is a social one—how kinsmen tend to be aligned genealogically in domestic units—and the consequent or dependent variable is a cultural one—rules of membership in descent groups.[24]

The other form of proposition is the reverse. The cultural principle serves as the antecedent or independent variable, and the extra-cultural condition serves as the consequent or dependent variable. Such propositions pertain to cultural forms as causes. An example is the proposition that different cultural standards for toilet training or weaning infants lead to types of experience that have different psychological consequences, creating different kinds of emotional problems and concerns (Whiting and Child 1953). To test this proposition we need to classify cultures according to their rules or standards governing toilet training and weaning, and we need to classify the associated populations according to the prevailing, relevant, emotional states of their members.

Whether the independent variable is the cultural or the extra-cultural one, the problems of classification for testing propositions are the same. To classify cultural forms we have to resort to the etic concepts with which we already describe and compare them. Our control over what we are doing depends on the ability of the etic concepts to describe the emic cultural forms under consideration, in all their variation. It also depends on the degree to which

24. Murdock (1949:59) tested the association of residence alignments with descent rules by using "rules of residence," citing Linton's (1936:169) suggestion that "Matrilineal descent is normally linked with matrilocal residence, patrilineal descent with patrilocal." But the status of Murdock's "rules of residence" as cultural rules governing residence decisions or as statistical norms relating to the alignment of kin in local groups and domestic units is not clear. He seems to have classified societies according to whichever type of information was available to him. Such inconsistency of procedure detracts from the evidence in support of the proposition to the extent that there is a discrepancy between cultural rules and the range and probability of variation in the alignments of kin that are their artifacts. For a further discussion of the problems in classifying residence forms, see Goodenough (1956b).

these etic concepts have themselves been systematized and ordered.

To classify extra-cultural conditions or the artifacts of cultural forms, we have to resort to whatever devices for measuring the variables in question the relevant sciences have developed. If the best measures we have of emotional climate are Rorschach and Thematic Apperception Tests, the kinds of propositions we can examine regarding emotional variables and the classifications we can make of them are limited by what we can measure with these tests and by their standard error in measuring it. If the social variables that interest us require precise demographic information of a particular kind we know how to get, we are still limited by the amount of information that has been reliably obtained for the societies available to us for comparative study.

We see, then, that comparative study of cultures and of the relations of cultural to extra-cultural phenomena is handicapped by the absence of emic ethnography and by the associated absence of satisfactory etic concepts. And we see that it is also handicapped by the absence of reliable information pertaining to the extra-cultural variables, even in the case of variables for which it is technically possible to get accurate information of the kind needed, as Ford (1966) also observed.

In actual practice, comparative study in anthropology often has been concerned with propositions about the relation of some extra-cultural conditions to other extra-cultural conditions, such as the relation of one kind of social condition to another or of an economic state of affairs to a social one. This is evident in Textor's (1967) compendium of "cross-cultural" findings. I must hasten to say that these extra-cultural conditions are often largely or entirely the product of human action that was itself informed and guided by the cultures of the actors. Propositions about such artifacts of culture often pertain indirectly, therefore, to the relations cultural forms have both to one another and to extra-cultural conditions. With care, they can be used as indirect tests of hypotheses regarding these relations. But we must recognize that what, in fact, are being classified and compared are not cultural forms, in the sense in which I have been speaking of culture. Rather, they are the material, social, and psychological artifacts of cultural forms.[25]

25. See, for example, many of the classifications in Murdock's (1967) *Ethnographic Atlas.*

An observation by Murdock (1949:214) will illustrate. He says,

> Where residence is matrilocal, a man in marrying rarely settles in a new community. He merely takes his possessions from his parents' home and moves, so to speak, across the street to that part of the same village where his wife and her relatives live. In only three of the 25 matrilocal and matrilineal societies in our sample is there evidence that a man commonly changes his community when he marries, and in one of these cases, the Dobuans, he regularly spends half of his time in his own village and only half in his wife's.

The proposition here is that in societies where the outcome of residence decisions associates the vast majority of married couples with the household with which the wife was already associated before marriage, the vast majority of married couples were already residents of the same community before their marriage.[26] The one variable—type of residence—has to do with statistical artifacts of whatever the cultural rules governing residence decisions happen to be. And somewhat different rules can produce similar artifacts.[27] The other variable—the frequency with which husband and wife come from the same community—also has to do with statistical artifacts of whatever are the cultural rules that govern the selection of spouses, which may allow for a narrow or very wide range of choice. A cultural rule that one must marry within one's community, if at all possible, is different from the statistical fact that most marriages are among people from the same community. Such a statistical fact is likely to result from such a cultural rule, but it

26. By "community," Murdock meant "the maximal group of persons who normally reside together in face-to-face association" (Murdock *et al.* 1945:29).

27. For example, where there are matrilineal corporations owning property, it may be a cultural rule that whenever landholdings and numbers of adult women permit, the women of a corporation should live together with their husbands on land subject to their corporation's control. On the other hand, where there are no matrilineal corporations owning property, there may be a rule that daughters have the duty to remain with their mothers after marriage; or the rule may be that a man has the duty of residing with and working for his wife's father or guardian. Any one of these different rules will tend to produce the kind of kin alignments in residential groups that anthropologists classify as matrilocal residence; but we are accustomed to speak of matrilocal residence as a "rule of residence" as if the matrilocal alignment were itself a cultural principle or the product of but one cultural principle.

may be a consequence of quite different considerations as well. The statistical fact is no sure indication of the underlying rule or principle.

Comparisons aimed at exploring the relations among extra-cultural variables are appropriate to a great many scientific objectives, as Ford (1966) has reminded us. And, as I have said, they can be used as indirect tests of hypotheses about strictly cultural variables. But we have often confused extra-cultural conditions with cultural forms, the artifacts of culture with culture, in comparative research. Thus we have failed to make explicit a major kind of imprecision in an endeavor already beset by other kinds of imprecision.[28]

Comparative study, then, requires that we have very clearly in mind just what kind of phenomena our theoretical interests are concerned with. Are we talking about culture, the artifacts of culture, or other extra-cultural conditions? What is the relationship of the variables we know how to measure (and for which classifications have been established in the context of other studies) to the variables that are our immediate theoretical concern? This question needs especially to be asked by those who are tempted to use the *Ethnographic Atlas* (Murdock 1967) and take its categories or codings as if they were relevant to any and all questions calling for comparative study. There are many occasions when resort to the *Ethnographic Atlas* will be appropriate, and a great many more when it may not be.

COMPARATIVE STUDY AND GENETIC RELATIONSHIP

There is a very different purpose for which comparison can be made, one that is concerned neither with propositions about the association of different cultural forms with one another within cultures nor with propositions about the relations of cultural forms to extra-cultural conditions. The purpose is to establish what cultures belong together as traditions deriving from a common ancestral culture, as related languages derive from a common ancestral language. It is possible, of course, for the several systems (or complexes, as they are often called) within a culture to have

28. For other kinds of imprecisions and problems in comparative research, see Naroll (1964, 1967), Legacé (1967), and Chaney and Ruiz Revilla (1969).

independent ancestries, as with language and religion in Anglo-American culture. Comparison with the object of establishing and tracing genetically related cultural systems was a major interest of anthropologists in the early decades of this century, as they tried to trace the origin and diffusion of particular traditions.[29]

The problem in such work is to identify the forms in one culture that are cognate with the forms in another related culture. Originally, before the separation of these cultures from their common source, there was a set of forms that functioned in particular ways. After separation, these forms gradually became modified independently in different ways in the daughter cultures. They were liable, also, to lose old functions and take on new ones. Some forms might be dropped entirely from the inventory of cultural resources and be replaced by other functionally competing forms, as was the technique of making fire by flint and steel in the United States.

There is an exact parallel in language. When a speech community divides into two distinct speech communities, the words in the once common language undergo subsequent modifications of phonic form independently; and they are liable to lose old meanings (functions) and acquire diverse new ones. It is well established that formal changes tend to be systematic. Thus, if there is a tendency for an initial p to shift to initial f in one word in a language, the tendency will apply to all words beginning with initial p in that language. Form is itself order. Change in form, insofar as it is a shift from one order to another and not simply a collapse into disorder, necessarily proceeds in an orderly manner. Such change is liable not to be noticed while it is going on because, at no point, does it entail any serious loss of formal order. People continue to understand one another, and individual variance remains within workable bounds.

As long as enough words in two related languages remain identifiably similar in form and function, a comparativist can use them to establish the fact of regular formal correspondence between the two languages in words of similar meaning, as is exemplified by Grimm's law (and its later refinements) for Indo-European lan-

29. The work of Wissler (1917, 1923, 1926) and Kroeber (1931, 1939, 1944, 1948) exemplifies this concern in American anthropology. See also the work of the German school of *Kulturkreislehre* (Kluckhohn 1936, Heine-Geldern 1964).

guages. Once it is clear that two languages are genetically related, further search begins to produce less obvious correspondences and to turn up words that are cognate in form but now rather divergent in meaning (e.g., English *queen* and Greek γυνή, "woman").

Nothing as neat as the Grimm's law kind of correspondence has been worked out for cultural forms other than linguistic ones. The closest anthropologists have come to a comparable degree of precision in establishing cognate forms has been in technology. As I said earlier, technology is a subject for which we have a long tradition of description that is how-to-do-it oriented. This orientation has required closer attention to emics and has led to a correspondingly refined development of etic concepts in this sector of culture. It is possible to equate technological "traits" according to similarities in both their formal organization and their function. By doing so, anthropologists and archaelogists have succeeded with a fair degree of precision in comparing technological systems with the object of determining what ones among them are related and what ones not.

But attempts to do this with other sectors of culture have been much less precise and often unconvincing. Where etics and emics are poorly developed, studies of the origin and spread of cultural forms have mistaken the rubrics of crude typologies of cultural artifacts—such as "megaliths," "pyramids," "patrilocal residence," and "Iroquois cousin terminology"—for the cultural forms themselves and have seen similarities of cultural form where often, in fact, there was none.

As will now be evident, even when we compare with an eye to finding cognate forms in different cultures, we start by resort to forms that are functionally analogous. If enough of them show similarities of form or regularities of difference in form to permit us to work out the patterns of formal correspondence, then we can make a case for formal and hence cultural cognation. But to develop our capacity to establish the cognation of cultural forms in other than language and technology, we must concentrate on emic description and on producing the refined etic concepts that come from attention to such description. Here, it seems to me, is where the study of cultural change and evolution has the most need for development and the most exciting and challenging possibilities for it.

CONCLUSION

So I have come back to etics and emics, again, to the interdependence of the general and the particular. And I have once again had occasion to mention the interdependence of formal and functional considerations in comparative study, considerations that must be kept clearly distinct in our minds so that we can deal with them satisfactorily in their interdependence. In all I have been saying, moreover, I have repeatedly emphasized the importance of our etic concepts for general science. At the same time, I have concurred with those who point to the futility of constructing typologies as ends in themselves, observing that how we are most suitably to classify both cultural forms and extra-cultural conditions for generalizing purposes depends on our theories and hypotheses and on what we think we are making generalizations about.

But is there not a contradiction here? What is a set of well-worked out etic concepts if not a typology? I have been emphasizing the need for satisfactory etics; I have devoted three earlier chapters to problems in the development of etic concepts in anthropology, all of which are definitions of types of something. Am I also saying there is no point in it all?

No, I am not. I have said that typologies are tools and that their adequacy has to be judged by the uses for which we design them. As a kind of typology, a systematized set of etic concepts is a tool for describing and comparing cultural forms. Its adequacy is judged by its ability satisfactorily to describe all the emic distinctions people actually make in all the world's cultures in relation to the subject matter (whether functionally or otherwise defined) for which the etic concepts were designed. And as it does so, it provides the materials from which various typologies of cultural forms can be constructed for specific investigative purposes. Such etic concepts satisfy the criteria for a comparative study of cultural forms free of ethnocentric or specific cultural bias.[30]

Something even more important derives from such etic concepts. If they embrace all of the distinctive features needed to describe the elementary emic units of any culture, they constitute the minimum number of concepts needed to determine empirically what are the universal attributes of culture and, by inference from them,

30. On this matter, see the similar remarks by Kluckhohn (1953:521).

the universal attributes of men as creators and users of cultures. Such universals help delineate the nature of the human species as such. To do this—apart from its historical and humanistic concerns—has been the principal scientific aim of anthropology.

In these chapters I have taken up some matters to which Lewis Henry Morgan long ago made pioneering contributions and have used them to illustrate the problems that beset this scientific endeavor. I have tried, also, to communicate the kind of thinking about these problems that I consider necessary if we are effectively to implement our purpose.

Appendix: Componential Analysis of the Kariera Kinship Terminology

As described by Radcliffe-Brown (Brown 1913), the Kariera have become a textbook example of a so-called four-section social system. Radcliffe-Brown presented them as organized into patrilineal descent groups. Each descent group was associated with a territory. The men of each group resided in its territory, where with their wives and children they formed a local group. The descent groups were exogamous and were aligned into two moieties, groups in óne moiety taking wives from groups in the other. Each moiety was subdivided into two sections, the sections named Karimera and Burung forming one moiety and those named Palyeri and Banaka forming the other. Karimera people could marry only generation mates in Palyeri, while Burung people could marry only generation mates in Banaka. A man's children were always in the section of his moiety other than his own, fathers and sons thus marrying into opposite sections of the other moiety. Radcliffe-Brown schematized the arrangement as shown in Figure 13.

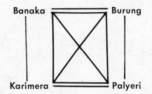

Figure 13. Radcliffe-Brown's model of cross-cousin marriage among the four Kariera sections. Double horizontal lines indicate marital ties; vertical lines indicate mother-child links; and diagonal lines indicate father-child links.

Radcliffe-Brown implied that preferred cross-cousin marriage combined with patrilineal clan exogamy had given rise to the moieties and sections. He saw the kinship terminology as reflecting the preference for cross-cousin marriage and the lines of patrilineal descent, and he diagrammed it accordingly (1930–31:49). Consequently, his diagram is a model of a closed system in which the two moieties are in balanced exchange. But in the next tribal area, into which the Kariera married, Radcliffe-Brown said that the sections, which had the same names, exchanged differently. One suspects that the system was less fixed and rigidly closed than Radcliffe-Brown's idealized model of it implies. Indeed, given a preference for brother-sister exchange in marriage, demographic fluctuations in the fairly small descent groups engaging in such exchanges would have required that each group maintain exchange relationships with several others at once. And from time to time radical rearrangements of exchange relationships would be necessary for at least some groups.

In a componential analysis of the Kariera kinship terms, Romney and Epling (1958) saw the section names as a product of the intersection of two basic discriminant variables. These variables were moiety membership and an odd–even alternation of generation. Ego's patrimoiety plus even generation made one section (Karimera in their example); ego's patrimoiety plus odd generation made another section (Burung); etc. They saw the kinship terms as classifying according to section, relative to ego's section, and according to generation seniority or generation difference within each section. A later analysis by Reid (1967) noted that for odd generations assignment of a relative to the older or younger generation depends on whether he is older or younger than ego. Otherwise his analysis closely parallels that of Romney and Epling in that it takes section membership as a basic criterion for the classification of kinsmen.

This works well for the kinship terms as used by a male ego alone or by female ego alone. But if one takes account of the closed reciprocal sets of terms, as one must in componential analysis (Goodenough 1965a, 1967), the use of section membership as a criterion proves unsatisfactory, resulting in some terms with disjunctive definitions and in loss of the integrity of the reciprocal sets. The terms for "son" and "daughter," which are the same for male and female ego, cut across section and moiety lines.

Another problem with existing analyses is acceptance of the assumption that because the section names go on alternating through the generations in each moiety, the kinship terminology must do likewise. Radcliffe-Brown assumed this and sought to elicit terms for the great-grandparent's and great-grandchild's generation. But he reported that there were no actual cases on record and that his exploration of hypothetical cases stopped with what he gave as the terms for father's father's father and father's father's mother, which he reported as *mainga* ("son") and *ngaraia* ("sister's daughter of a man" and "son's wife") respectively, thus seeming to confirm the idea of an alternation of kinship terms corresponding with the alternation of section names.

But if one asks what an ego calls his father's *maeli* ("father's father"), one is also referring to his father's "son's son" (ego's own son or his brother's son). Thus one invites the answer *mainga* ("son"). And if one asks ego what he calls the wife of this *mainga,* one invites the answer *ngaraia,* because that is what one calls the wife of any of one's *mainga.* Thus a question by the ethnographer aiming at the second ascending generation from ego's father may well have been understood by the informant as aiming at the second descending generation from ego's father, for father's father and son's son are classed together as the same kind of kinsman.

This observation would be a mere quibble on my part were it not that the kinship terminology exhibits features suggesting that it does not extend beyond the second ascending and descending generations. (Such would account for Radcliffe-Brown's apparent difficulty in getting information by way of hypothetical cases.) The section names may go on alternating down through the generations, but the kinship terms, it would appear, do not. To be sure, the same terms are used in the grandparents' and grandchildren's generations, but they are not used in the same way in these generations. One must know which party is senior and what his or her sex is in order to make sense of the terms, a fact Radcliffe-Brown discussed at length. Seniority also plays a role in the classification of relatives in the first ascending and descending generations, and Radcliffe-Brown was explicit that a relative in either of these generations was assigned to the senior or junior one according to whether he was older or younger than ego by birth order without regard to actual generation membership. Thus a brother's son was classed with ego's father and father's brother if he was older than ego. For this reason, Reid (1967) referred to the generations as "pseudo-generations." The implication is clear that surviving members of the third ascending generation were assimilated on account of age to the first ascending generation and not to the first descending generation, as Radcliffe-Brown's too limited inquiry led him to believe. I do not see how seniority can function as a criterion for classifying relationships in other generations if, at the same time, these generations alternate indefinitely in a leap-frog manner without regard to which is senior and which junior. I must conclude, therefore, that Radcliffe-Brown was mistaken in this case, basing his conclusion on insufficient and misleading evidence and on the example of what was held to be true of some other Australian tribes. If, as componential analysis reveals, section membership is not a necessary criterion of Kariera kinship classification, then we can treat the Kariera terminology as we would any other that extends only two generations distant from ego (e.g., that of Moala in Fiji).

THE KINSHIP DATA

The terms listed below are those reported by Radcliffe-Brown (Brown 1913). They are arranged in groups of closed sets of reciprocal terms, each set being given a letter. Denotata not inclosed in brackets are those reported by Radcliffe-Brown.[1] Those in brackets are additional examples I have added on the basis of Radcliffe-Brown's model of the system. The relationships in the lists of denotata are diagrammed in Figures 14–16.

A. *kaja:* (older than ego) B, FBS, MZS, [FFBSS, MMZDS, MFZSS, FMBDS, FFZDS, MFMBSSS, WZH, HZH, FFMBSDS, MFFZSSS, FFBWBDS, MFZHBSS].
   margara: (younger than ego) as with *kaja*.
   turdu: (older than ego) Z, FBD, MZD, [FFBSD, MMZDD, MFZSD, FMBDD, FFZDD, MFMBSSD, WBW, HBW, HW, FFMBSDD, MFFZSSD, FFBWBDD, MFZHBSD].
   mari: (younger than ego) as with *turdu*.
B. *kumbali:* (male ego) MBS, FZS, WB, ZH, [MMBDS, MFZDS, FMZDS, MMZSS, MFBSS, FFBDS, WFBS, FBDH, WMZS, MZDH, WFZDH].
C. *bungali:* (female ego) MBD, FZD, HZ, BW, [MMBDD, MFZDD, FMZDD, MMZSD, MFBSD, FFBDD, HFBD, FBSW, HMZD, MZSW, HFZSW].
D. *ñuba:* (male ego) MBD, FZD, W, WZ, BW, [MMBDD, MFZDD, FMZDD, MMZSD, MFBSD, FFBDD, WFZSW, WFBD, FBSW, WMZD, MZSW]; (female ego) MBS, FZS, H, HB, ZH, [MMBDS, MFZDS, MMZSS, MFBSS, FFBDS, HMBDH, FBDH, HFBS, MZDH, HMZS].
   nguranu:[2] (male ego) W, a female *ñuba* a male ego has married.
   yarungu:[2] (male ego) BW, a female *ñuba* a man other than ego has married.
E. *mama:* F, FB, MZH, WMB, HMB, MBWB, ZHMB, [FFBS, MFZS, MFFBDS, FMMBSS, MMFZDS, FMFZSS], H of any *nganga*.
   nganga: M, MZ, FBW, WFZ, HFZ, [MMZD, MFBD, FMMZSD, MFFZDD, MMFZSD, MFMBDD, FFFZSD], W of any *mama*.

1. Symbols used for the denotata of the terms are: B, brother; D, daughter; F, father; H, husband; M, mother; S, son; W, wife; Z, sister. Thus FMBWZS is to be read "father's mother's brother's wife's sister's son."
2. Because the terms *nguranu* and *yarungu* designate subsets of the set of denotata designated by *ñuba*, I do not consider them in the analysis.

mainga: (male ego) S, BS, FFF,[3] [FBSS, MBDS, MFBSDS, FFSDSS, MMFDDS, FMBDSS, S of any *kaja* or *margara*]; (female ego) S, ZS, [MZDS, FBDS, FZSS, FMZDSS, MMBSDS, FMBDDS, MFZSDS, FMBSSS, S of any *turdu* or *mari.*

kundal: (male ego) D, BD, [FBSD, MBDD, MFBZDD, FFSDSD, MMFDDD, FMBDSD, D of any *kaja* or *margara*]; (female ego) D, ZD, [MZDD, FBDD, FZSD, FMZDSD, MMBZDD, FMBDDD, MFZSDD, FMBSSD, D of any *turdu* or *mari*].

F. *kaga:* MB, FZH, WF, HF, [MMZS, MFBS, MFMBDS, MFFBSS, FMMZSS, FMFBSS, FBWB, H of any female *toa* or *yuro*].

yuro: (female ego) FZ, MBW, HM [FFBD, MFZD, FMFZSD, MMMZSD, MFFBDD, MFMZDD, W of any *kaga*].

kuling: (male ego) ZS, DH, [MZDS, FBDS, FZSS, MFZSDS, FFBSDS, FMZDSS, FFBDSS, ZHBS, H of any *kundal*].

ngaraia (male ego) ZD, SW, FFM,[3] [MZDD, FBDD, FZSD, MFZSDD, FFBZDD, FMZDSD, FFBDSD, ZHBD, W of any *mainga*]; (female ego) BD, SW, [FBSD, MZSD, FMBDSD, FMZDDD, MFBZDD, MMZSDD, MBDD, W of any *mainga*].

bali: (male ego) as with *ngaraia.*

G. *toa:* (male ego) FZ, MBW, HM, [FFBD, FMZD, MFZD, FMFZSD, MMMZSD, MFFBDD, MFMZDD, W of any *kaga*]; (female ego) BS, DH, HZS, [FBSS, MZSS, FMBDSS, FMZDDS, MFBSDS, MMZSDS, MBDS, H of any *kundal*].

H. *yumani:* same as *toa* after extreme avoidance tabus have been lifted.

I. *maeli:* (male or female ego) FF, FFB, MMB, WMF, HMF, [any *kaja* or *margara* of FF or MM, any *ñuba* of FM, any *kumbali* of MF]; (male ego) SS, SD, [BSS, BSD, ZDS, ZDD, SS or SD of any *kaja* or *margara,* DS or DD of any *turdu* or *mari,* SS or SD of any *ñuba,* DS or DD of any *kumbali*].

---

3. The denotata FFF for *mainga* and FFM for *ngaraia* are not considered in the analysis for reasons given in the text.

J. *kandari:* (male or female ego) MM, MMZ, FFZ, WFM, HFM, [any *turdu* or *mari* of MM or FF, any *ñuba* of MF, any *bungali* of FM]; (female ego) DS, DD, [BSS, BSD, DS or DD of any *turdu* or *mari,* SS or SD of any *kaja* or *margara,* SS or SD of any *bungali,* DS or DD of any *ñuba*].

K. *tami:* (male or female ego) MF, MFB, FMB, HFF, WFF, [any *kaja* or *margara* of MF or FM, any *ñuba* of MM, any *kumbali* of FF, FF of any *ñuba* or *kumbali* or *bungali*]; (male ego) DS, DD, [ZSS, ZSD, DS or DD of any *kaja* or *margara,* SS or SD of any *turdu* or *mari.* SS or SD of any *ñuba,* DS or DD of any *kumbali*].

L. *kabali:* (male or female ego) FM, FMZ, MFZ, WMM, HMM, [any *turdu* or *mari* of FM or MF, any *ñuba* of FF, any *bungali* of MM, MM of any *ñuba* or *kumbali* or *bungali*]; (female ego) SS, SD, [ZSS, ZSD, BDS, BDD, SS or SD of any *turdu* or *mari,* DS or DD of any *kaja* or *margara,* DS or DD of any *bungali,* SS or SD of any *ñuba*].

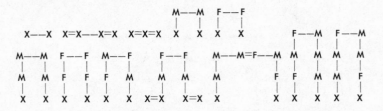

kaja, margara, turdu, mari — kaja, margara, turdu, mari

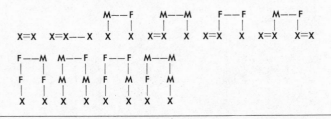

kumbali — kumbali, bungali — bungali, ñuba — ñuba

Figure 14. The A, B, C, D sets of relationships.

Figure 15. The E, F, G, H sets of relationships.

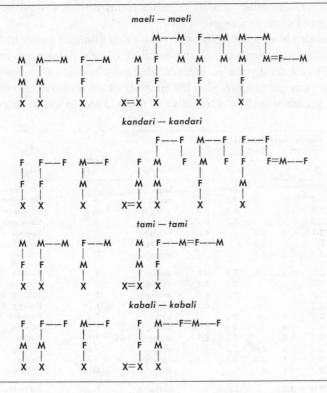

Figure 16. The I, J, K, L sets of relationships.

ANALYSIS

Several different analyses are possible, involving the selection of different discriminant variables as criteria of classification.

We can use alter's being in an odd or even generation in relation to ego's generation, for example. We must then add as an additional variable alter's being in the same generation with ego or in a different one, in order to distinguish the terms in sets I, J, K, and L from those in sets A, B, C, and D, all of which are in even generations. We can also replace these two variables, as I do here, with a single variable of degree of generation distance between ego and alter, assuming that the kinship terms do not extend beyond two generations from ego.

We also have a choice between two other complex variables. One is oddness or evenness of the number of sex differences among coeval collateral pairs in the genealogical chain in other than terminal even generations plus the number of marital ties in terminal even generations. The alternative is the oddness or evenness of the

	Discriminant Variables						Recip.	
1	2	3	4	5	6	Kin term	set	Section*
1.0	2.0	...	...	5.0	6.0	kaja	A	Karimera
1.0	2.0	...	...	5.0	6.1	turdu	A	Karimera
1.0	2.0	...	...	5.1	6.0	margara	A	Karimera
1.0	2.0	...	...	5.1	6.1	mari	A	Karimera
1.0	2.1	...	4.0	...	6.0	kumbali	B	Palyeri
1.0	2.1	...	4.0	...	6.1	bungali	C	Palyeri
1.0	2.1	...	4.1	...	...	ñuba	D	Palyeri
1.1	2.0	...	...	5.0	6.0	mama	E	Burung
1.1	2.0	...	...	5.0	6.1	nganga	E	Banaka
1.1	2.0	...	...	5.1	6.0	maiñga	E	Burung, Banaka
1.1	2.0	...	...	5.1	6.1	kundal	E	Burung, Banaka
1.1	2.1	3.0	...	5.0	...	kaga	F-1	Banaka
1.1	2.1	3.0	...	5.1	6.0	kuling	F-1	Banaka
1.1	2.1	3.0	...	5.1	6.1	ngaraia₁, bali	F-1	Banaka
1.1	2.1	3.1	4.0	5.0	...	yuro	F-2	Burung
1.1	2.1	3.1	4.0	5.1	...	ngaraia₂	F-2	Burung
1.1	2.1	3.1	4.1	...	...	toa, yumani	G, H	Burung
1.2	2.0	3.0	...	...	...	maeli	I	Karimera
1.2	2.0	3.1	...	...	...	kandari	J	Karimera
1.2	2.1	3.0	...	...	...	tami	K	Palyeri
1.2	2.1	3.1	...	...	...	kabali	L	Palyeri

* Sections distribute assuming that ego is Karimera.

Variables:
1. Degree of generation distance between ego and alter: 1.0 same generation, 1.1 one generation distant, 1.2 two generations distant.
2. Number of sex differences among coeval collateral pairs in other than terminal even generations plus number of marital ties in terminal even generations OR number of cross-sex parent-child ties descending from even to odd generations plus number of marital ties in even generations (assuming generation of junior party is always even): 2.0 number even, 2.1 number odd.
3. Sex of the senior party: 3.0 senior party male, 3.1 senior party female.
4. Presence of sex difference between ego and alter: 4.0 sex difference absent, 4.1 sex difference present.
5. Age of alter relative to ego: 5.0 alter older, 5.1 alter younger.
6. Sex of alter: 6.0 alter male, 6.1 alter female.

Figure 17. Componential matrix of Kariera kinship terms.

number of cross-sex parent-child links descending from even to odd generations plus the number of marital ties in even generations in the genealogical chain (cf. Kay 1965). In the latter case, the generation of the junior party to the relationship is the point of reference and is regarded as even. Figure 17 presents the variables and results of my analysis in the form of a matrix table.

CONCLUSION

The analysis shows that sections are not necessary for understanding the kinship terminology. It can be understood in terms of various applications of the elemental idea of odd/even, imbalance/balance, or asymmetry/symmetry (however one wishes to phrase it) in relation to generation, sex differences, and marital ties.[4] The Kariera also had named sections, and the kinship terminology for any ego distributes neatly according to section from the point of view of his or her sex. To ask whether the Kariera thought of it in terms of odd or even or in terms of section membership assumes erroneously that people have only one model for understanding something and only one way of thinking about it. The Kariera probably conceived of it in both ways. Different modes of reckoning that produce the same results make it possible for people to draw inferences from limited information, employing whatever model can allow for valid inference from the information available. And people are continually having to interpret events in accordance with a cultural design on the basis of limited information.

Our analysis makes it clear, however, that neither the sections nor preference for cross-cousin marriage in brother-sister exchange are necessarily antecedent to the kinship terminology, however well they fit with it. One can easily see how the section names provide a simple mode of reckoning how descent groups stand to one another at any particular time in relation to marital exchanges; and it is not improbable that the system of marital exchange gave rise to the alignment of descent groups in moieties or apparent moieties, within a region, according to their overlapping, multiple arrange-

4. Such elemental ideas are, of course, in themselves aspects of what Lévi-Strauss (1949:107) has referred to as "les notions d'opposition et de corrélation" that he regarded as fundamental to the dualistic principle.

ments for exchange. If a man of *A* has a wife from *B* and a man from *C* has that woman's "sister" for his wife, then a generation of group *A* and a generation of group *C* stand in a symmetrical relationship to a generation of group *B* and are "brothers." Where continuing arrangements for exchange marriages are preferred down through the generations, such "brother" relationships tend to last through time and, within restricted areas, to align descent groups into "our side" as against the "other side" in a network of exchange relationships, such as Radcliffe-Brown has described for the Kariera (Brown 1913). Awareness of this and use of the awareness as a quick way of reckoning how people stand to one another could easily lead to formalization, with the named sections a result.

Thus it was reasonable for Radcliffe-Brown (1930-31) to attribute moieties (both explicit and implicit) and named sections (where they occur) to the pattern of intergroup relationships resulting from marriage customs in Australia. But it was preference for marital exchanges, not a preferred cross-cousin marriage *per se,* that was involved. We must agree with Lévi-Strauss (1949) that exchange relationships were fundamental here. But we cannot conclude, for the Kariera at least, that the kinship terminology is a creature of these exchanges in the same way the sections and moieties are, however much it may have been influenced by them. It can be understood independently.

References

Aaby, Peter S.
  1970. The Criterion of Polarity. *American Anthropologist,* vol. 72, pp. 349–351.
Aberle, David F.
  1953. *The Kinship System of the Kalmuk Mongols.* University of New Mexico Publications in Anthropology No. 8.
  1967. A Scale of Alternate Generation Terminology. *Southwestern Journal of Anthropology,* vol. 23, pp. 261–276.
Aberle, David F., *et al.*
  1963. The Incest Taboo and the Mating Patterns of Animals. *American Anthropologist,* vol. 65, pp. 253–265.
Adams, Richard N.
  1960. An Inquiry into the Nature of the Family. In G. E. Dole and R. L. Carneiro, eds., *Essays in the Science of Society in Honor of Leslie A. White,* pp. 30–49. New York: Thomas Y. Crowell.
Adelman, Fred
  1954. *The Kalmuks of the Lower Volga Region and Their Kinship Structure.* Unpublished M.A. thesis, University of Pennsylvania.
Aiyappan, A.
  1945. *Iravas and Culture Change.* Bulletin of the Madras Government Museum, N.S. General Section, vol. 5, no. 1.
Atkins, John R., and Luke Curtis
  1968. Game Rules and the Rules of Culture. In I. R. Buchler and H. G. Nutini, eds., *Game Theory in the Behavioral Sciences,* pp. 213–234. Pittsburgh: University of Pittsburgh Press.
Barnes, J. A.
  1958. Kinship. *Encyclopædia Britannica,* vol. 13, pp. 403–409.

1961. Physical and Social Kinship. *Philosophy of Science,* vol. 28, pp. 296–299.

1962. African Models in the New Guinea Highlands. *Man,* vol. 62, pp. 5–9.

1964. Physical and Social Facts in Social Anthropology. *Philosophy of Science,* vol. 31, pp. 294–297.

Barnett, H. G.

1949. *Palauan Society.* Eugene: University of Oregon Publications.

Barth, Fredrik

1966. *Models of Social Organization.* Royal Anthropological Institute Occasional Paper No. 23. London: Royal Anthropological Institute of Great Britain and Ireland.

Barton, R. F.

1949. *The Kalingas: Their Institutions and Custom Law.* Chicago: University of Chicago Press.

Bell, Norman W., and Ezra F. Vogel, eds.

1960. *A Modern Introduction to the Family.* New York: Free Press.

Berlin, Brent, Dennis E. Breedlove, and Peter H. Raven

1968. Covert Categories and Folk Taxonomies. *American Anthropologist,* vol. 70, pp. 290–299.

Bloch, Bernard, and George L. Trager

1942. *Outline of Linguistic Analysis.* Special Publications of the Linguistic Society of America.

Bohannan, Paul

1963. *Social Anthropology.* New York: Holt, Rinehart and Winston.

Bollig, Laurentius

1927. *Die Bewohner der Truk-Inseln.* Anthropos Internationale Sammlung Ethnologischer Monographien, vol. 3, no. 1. Münster i. W.: Aschendorffsche Verlagsbuchhandlung.

Brown (Radcliffe-Brown), A. R.

1913. Three Tribes of Western Australia. *Journal of the Royal Anthropological Institute,* vol. 43 (n.s. vol. 16), pp. 143–194.

Brown, Paula

1962. Non-Agnates among the Patrilineal Chimbu. *Journal of the Polynesian Society,* vol. 71, pp. 57–69.

Buchler, Ira R.

1966. On Physical and Social Kinship. *Anthropological Quarterly,* vol. 39, pp. 17–15.

Buchler, Ira R., and Henry A. Selby

1968. *Kinship and Social Organization: An Introduction to Theory and Method.* New York: Macmillan.

Buck, Peter H. (Te Rangi Hiroa)

1930. *Samoan Material Culture.* Bernice P. Bishop Museum Bulletin No. 75.

1944. *Arts and Crafts of the Cook Islands.* Bernice P. Bishop Museum Bulletin No. 179.

Burling, Robbins

1969. Linguistics and Ethnographic Description. *American Anthropologist,* vol. 71, pp. 817–827.

Carroll, Vern, ed.

1970. *Adoption in Eastern Oceania.* Honolulu: University of Hawaii Press.

Casagrande, Joseph B.

1963. Language Universals in Anthropological Perspective. In J. H. Greenberg, ed., *Universals of Language,* pp. 220–235. Cambridge, Mass.: M.I.T. Press.

Chaney, Richard P., and Rogelio Ruiz Revilla

1969. Sampling Methods and Interpretation of Correlation: A Comparative Analysis of Seven Cross-Cultural Samples. *American Anthropologist,* vol. 71, pp. 597–633.

Chowning, Ann

1962. Cognatic Groups among the Molima of Fergusson Island. *Ethnology,* vol. 1, pp. 92–101.

1966. Lakalai Kinship. *Anthropological Forum,* vol. 1, pp. 476–501.

Chowning, Ann, and Ward H. Goodenough

1966. Lakalai Political Organization. *Anthropological Forum,* vol. 1, pp. 412–473.

Clarke, Edith

1957. *My Mother Who Fathered Me.* London: George Allen and Unwin.

Cohen, Yehudi

1956. Structure and Function: Family Organization and Socialization in a Jamaican Community. *American Anthropologist,* vol. 58, pp. 664–686.

Davenport, William H.

1959. Nonunilinear Descent and Descent Groups. *American Anthropologist,* vol. 61, pp. 557–572.

1961. The Family System of Jamaica. *Social and Economic Studies,* vol. 10, pp. 420–454.

1963. Social Organization. In B. J. Siegel, ed., *Biennial Review of Anthropology,* pp. 178–227. Stanford: Stanford University Press.

1964. Social Structure of Santa Cruz Islands. In W. H. Goodenough, ed., *Explorations in Cultural Anthropology: Essays in Honor of George Peter Murdock*, pp. 57–93. New York: McGraw-Hill.

Davis, Kingsley, and Lloyd Warner
    1937. Structural Analysis of Kinship. *American Anthropologist*, vol. 39, pp. 291–313.

de Lepervanche, Marie
    1967–68. Descent, Residence and Leadership in the New Guinea Highlands. *Oceania*, vol. 38, pp. 134–158, 163–189.

Dyen, Isidore
    1949. On the History of the Trukese Vowels. *Language*, vol. 25, pp. 420–436.

Eggan, Fred
    1968. Kinship: Introduction. *International Encyclopedia of the Social Sciences*, vol. 8, pp. 390–401. New York: Macmillan and Free Press.

Ember, Melvin
    1959. The Nonunilineal Descent Groups of Samoa. *American Anthropologist*, vol. 61: pp. 573–577.

Evans-Pritchard, E. E.
    1940. *The Nuer*. Oxford: Clarendon Press.
    1951. *Kinship and Marriage among the Nuer*. Oxford: Clarendon Press.

Firth, Raymond
    1936. *We the Tikopia*. London: George Allen and Unwin.
    1957. A Note on Descent Groups in Polynesia. *Man*, vol. 57, pp. 4–8.
    1963. Bilateral Descent Groups, An Operational Viewpoint. In I. Schaperia, ed., *Studies in Kinship and Marriage*. Royal Anthropological Institute Occasional Paper No. 16. London: Royal Anthropological Institute of Great Britain and Ireland.

Fischer, J. L.
    1960. Genealogical Space. *Oceania*, vol. 30, pp. 181–187.

Ford, Clellan S.
    1966. On the Analysis of Behavior for Cross-Cultural Comparisons. *Behavior Science Notes*, vol. 1, pp. 79-97.

Forde, Daryll
    1963. On Some Further Unconsidered Aspects of Descent. *Man*, vol. 63, pp. 12–13.

Fortes, Meyer
    1945. *The Dynamics of Clanship among the Tallensi*. London: Oxford University Press.

1949. *The Web of Kinship among the Tallensi.* London: Oxford University Press.

1953. The Structure of Unilineal Descent Groups. *American Anthropologist,* vol. 55, pp. 17–41.

1959. Descent, Filiation and Affinity. *Man,* vol. 59, pp. 193–197, 206–212.

1962. Introduction. In M. Fortes, ed., *Marriage in Tribal Societies,* pp. 1–13. Cambridge Papers in Social Anthropology No. 3.

Fox, Robin
1967. *Kinship and Marriage.* Baltimore: Penguin Books.

1968. The Evolution of Human Sexual Behavior. *The New York Times Magazine,* March 24, pp. 32–33, 79–97.

Freedman, Maurice
1958. *Lineage Organization in Southeastern China.* London School of Economics Monographs on Social Anthropology No. 18. London: Athlone Press.

1966. *Chinese Lineage and Society: Fukien and Kwangtung.* London School of Economics Monographs on Social Anthropology No. 33. London: Athlone Press.

Freeman, J. D.
1958. The Family System of the Iban of Borneo. In J. Goody, ed., *The Developmental Cycle in Domestic Groups,* pp. 15–52. Cambridge Papers in Social Anthropology No. 1. Cambridge University Press.

1961. On the Concept of the Kindred. *Journal of the Royal Anthropological Institute,* vol. 91, pp. 192–220.

Glasse, R. M.
1959. The Huli Descent System: A Preliminary Account. *Oceania,* vol. 29, pp. 171–183.

Gluckman, Max
1950. Kinship and Marriage among the Lozi of Northern Rhodesia and the Zulu of Natal. In A. R. Radcliffe-Brown and D. Forde, eds., *African Systems of Kinship and Marriage,* pp. 166–206. London: Oxford University Press.

Goodale, Jane C.
1959. *The Tiwi Women of Melville Island, North Australia.* Ph.D. Dissertation, University of Pennsylvania (University Microfilm Libraries, Inc.).

1962. Marriage Contracts among the Tiwi. *Ethnology,* vol. 1, pp. 452–466.

Goode, William J.
1964. *The Family.* Englewood Cliffs, N. J.: Prentice-Hall.

148 *Description and Comparison in Cultural Anthropology*

1966. Note on Problems in Theory and Method: The New World. *American Anthropologist*, vol. 68, pp. 486–492.

Goodenough, Ward H.

1951. *Property, Kin, and Community on Truk.* Yale University Publications in Anthropology No. 46.

1955. A Problem in Malayo-Polynesian Social Organization. *American Anthropologist*, vol. 57, pp. 71–83.

1956a. Componential Analysis and the Study of Meaning. *Language*, vol. 32, pp. 195–216.

1956b. Residence Rules. *Southwestern Journal of Anthropology*, vol. 12, pp. 22–37.

1961a. Review of *Social Structure in Southeast Asia. American Anthropologist*, vol. 63, pp. 1341–1347.

1961b. Comments on Cultural Evolution. *Daedalus,* vol. 90, pp. 521–528.

1962. Kindred and Hamlet in Lakalai, New Britain. *Ethnology*, vol. 1, pp. 5–12.

1963. *Cooperation in Change.* New York: Russell Sage Foundation.

1964. Componential Analysis of Könkämä Lapp Kinship Terminology. In W. H. Goodenough, ed., *Explorations in Cultural Anthropology: Essays in Honor of George Peter Murdock,* pp. 221–238. New York: McGraw-Hill.

1965a. Yankee Kinship Terminology: A Problem in Componential Analysis. In E. A. Hammel, ed., *Formal Semantic Analysis,* pp. 269–287. Special Publication, *American Anthropologist*, vol. 67, no. 5, part 2.

1965b. Personal Names and Modes of Address in Two Oceanic Societies. In M. E. Spiro, ed., *Context and Meaning in Cultural Anthropology,* pp. 265–276. New York: Free Press.

1967. Componential Analysis. *Science,* vol. 156, pp. 1203–1209.

1968. Componential Analysis. *International Encyclopedia of the Social Sciences,* vol. 3, pp. 186–192. New York: Macmillan and Free Press.

1969. Frontiers of Cultural Anthropology: Social Organization. *Proceedings of the American Philosophical Society,* vol. 113, pp. 329–335.

Goody, Jack

1956. A Comparative Approach to Incest and Adultery. *British Journal of Sociology,* vol. 7, pp. 286–304.

1961. The Classification of Double Descent Systems. *Current Anthropology,* vol. 2, pp. 3–25.

1968. Kinship: Descent Groups. *International Encyclopedia of the Social Sciences,* vol. 8, pp. 401–408. New York: Macmillan and Free Press.

1969. Adoption in Cross-Cultural Perspective. *Comparative Studies in Society and History,* vol. 11, pp. 55–78.

Gough, Kathleen
1959. The Nayars and the Definition of Marriage. *Journal of the Royal Anthropological Institute,* vol. 89, pp. 23–34.
1961. Nayar: Central Kerala. In D. M. Schneider and K. Gough, eds., *Matrilineal Kinship,* pp. 298–384. Berkeley and Los Angeles: University of California Press.

Gould, Nathan
1963. Functionalism as Rationalization: An Analysis of Ethnocentric Bias in Anthropological Inquiry. *Anthropological Quarterly,* vol. 39, pp. 225–264.

Gray, Robert F.
1960. Sonjo Bride-Price and the Question of African "Wife-Purchase." *American Anthropologist,* vol. 62, pp. 34–57.

Greenberg, Joseph H.
1963. *Universals of Language.* Cambridge, Mass.: M.I.T. Press.
1966. Language Universals. In T. A. Sebeok, ed., *Current Trends in Linguistics,* vol. 3: *Theoretical Foundations,* pp. 61–112. The Hague: Mouton.

Grimes, Joseph E., and Barbara E. Grimes
1962. Semantic Distinctions in Huichol (Uto-Aztecan) Kinship. *American Anthropologist,* vol. 64, pp. 104–114.

Groves, Murray
1963a. Western Motu Descent Groups. *Ethnology,* vol. 2, pp. 15–30.
1963b. The Nature of Fijian Society. *Journal of the Polynesian Society,* vol. 72, pp. 272–291.

Harris, Marvin
1964. *The Nature of Cultural Things.* New York: Random House.
1968. *The Rise of Anthropological Theory.* New York: Thomas Y. Crowell.

Heine-Geldern, Robert
1964. One Hundred Years of Ethnological Theory in the German Speaking Countries. *Current Anthropology,* vol. 5, pp. 407–418.

Helm, June
1965. Bilaterality in the Socio-Territorial Organization of the Arctic Drainage Dene. *Ethnology,* vol. 4, pp. 361–385.

Herskovits, Melville J.
　1938. *Dahomey: An Ancient West Africa Kingdom.* 2 vols. New
　　York: J. J. Augustin.
Hoenigswald, Henry M.
　1960. *Language Change and Linguistic Reconstruction.* Chicago:
　　University of Chicago Press.
Hohfeld, Wesley N.
　1919. *Fundamental Legal Concepts.* New Haven: Yale University
　　Press.
Holmberg, Allan R.
　1950. *Nomads of the Long Bow.* Smithsonian Institution, Institute
　　of Social Anthropology, Publication No. 10.
Homans, George C.
　1941. *English Villagers of the Thirteenth Century.* Cambridge, Mass.:
　　Harvard University Press.
Jeffreys, M. D. W.
　1951. Lobolo is Child-Price. *African Studies,* vol. 10, pp. 145–184.
Junod, Henri A.
　1927. *The Life of a South African Tribe.* 2nd ed., 2 vols. London:
　　Macmillan.
Kay, Paul
　1965. A Generalization of the Cross/Parallel Distinction. *American
　　Anthropologist,* vol. 67, pp. 30–43.
Keesing, Roger M.
　1966. Kwaio Kindreds. *Southwestern Journal of Anthropology,* vol.
　　22, pp. 346–353.
　1968. Nonunilineal Descent and Contextual Definition of Status:
　　The Kwaio Evidence. *American Anthropologist,* vol. 70, pp.
　　82–84.
　1970a. Shrines, Ancestors, and Nonunilineal Descent: The Kwaio
　　and Tallensi. *American Anthropologist,* vol. 72 (in press).
　1970b. Kwaio Fosterage. *American Anthropologist,* vol. 72 (in
　　press).
Kennedy, Raymond
　1937. A Survey of Indonesian Civilization. In G. P. Murdock, ed.,
　　Studies in the Science of Society, pp. 267–297. New Haven: Yale
　　University Press.
Kirchhoff, Paul
　1932. Verwandtschaftsbezeichnungen und Verwandtenheirat. *Zeit-
　　schrift für Ethnologie,* vol. 64, pp. 41–71.

Kluckhohn, Clyde
1936. Some reflections on the Method and Theory of Kultur-kreislehre. *American Anthropologist*, vol. 38, pp. 157–196.
1953. Universal Categories of Culture. In A. L. Kroeber *et al.*, eds., *Anthropology Today: An Encyclopedic Inventory*, pp. 507–523. Chicago: University of Chicago Press.

Kopytoff, Igor
1964. Family and Lineage among the Suku of the Congo. In R. F. Gray and P. H. Gulliver, eds., *The Family Estate in Africa*, pp. 83–116. London: Routledge and Kegan Paul.

Kroeber, A. L.
1909. Classificatory Systems of Relationship. *Journal of the Royal Anthropological Institute*, vol. 39, pp. 77–84.
1931. The Culture-Area and Age-Area Concepts of Clark Wissler. In S. Rice, ed., *Methods in Social Science—A Case Book*, pp. 248–265. Chicago: University of Chicago Press.
1939. *Cultural and Natural Areas of Native North America.* University of California Publications in American Achaeology and Ethnology, vol. 38.
1944. *Configurations of Culture Growth.* Berkeley: University of California Press.
1948. *Anthropology.* New ed., rev. New York: Harcourt, Brace.

Kroeber, A. L., and Clyde Kluckhohn
1952. *Culture: A Critical Review of Concepts and Definitions.* Papers of the Peabody Museum of Archaeology and Ethnology, vol. 47, no. 1.

Kutsche, Paul
1960. Land Inheritance and Kinship Structure: The Eastern Kentucky Deme. Unpublished paper read at the Colorado-Wyoming Academy of Science, Boulder.

Lambert, Bernd
1966. Ambilineal Descent Groups in the Northern Gilbert Islands. *American Anthropologist*, vol. 68, pp. 641–664.

Langness, L. L.
1964. Some Problems in the Conceptualization of Highlands Social Structure. In J. B. Watson, ed., *New Guinea: The Central Highlands*, pp. 162–182. Special Publication, *American Anthropologist*, vol. 66, no. 4, part 2.

Leach, Edmund R.
1950. *Social Science Research in Sarawak.* Colonial Research Studies No. 1. London: His Majesty's Stationery Office.

1955. Polyandry, Inheritance, and the Definition of Marriage: With Particular Reference to Sinhalese Customary Law. *Man*, vol. 55, pp. 182–186.

1961. *Rethinking Anthropology*. London School of Economics Monographs on Social Anthropology No. 22. London: Athlone Press.

1962. On Some Unconsidered Aspects of Double Descent Systems. *Man*, vol. 62, pp. 130–134.

√ Legacé, Robert O.
1967. Principles and Procedures of Ethnic Unit Identification. *Behavior Science Notes*, vol. 2, pp. 89–100.

Lévi-Strauss, Claude
1949. *Les structures élémentaires de la parenté*. Paris: Presses universitaires de France.

Levy, M. J., Jr., and L. A. Fallers
1959. The Family: Some Comparative Considerations. *American Anthropologist*, vol. 61, pp. 647–651.

Linton, Ralph
1936. *The Study of Man*. New York: Appleton-Century-Crofts.

Lloyd, P. C.
1966. Agnatic and Cognatic Descent among the Yoruba. *Man*, n.s., vol. 1, pp. 483–500.

Lounsbury, Floyd G.
√ 1953. Field Methods and Techniques in Linguistics. In A. L. Kroeber et al., *Anthropology Today: An Encyclopedic Inventory*, pp. 401–416. Chicago: University of Chicago Press.

1956. A Semantic Analysis of the Pawnee Kinship Usage. *Language*, vol. 32, pp. 158–194.

1963. Linguistics and Psychology. In S. Koch, ed., *Psychology: A Study of Science*, vol. 6, pp. 552–582. New York: McGraw-Hill.

√ 1964a. The Structural Analysis of Kinship Semantics. In H. G. Lunt, ed., *Proceedings of the Ninth International Congress of Linguists*, pp. 1073–1093. The Hague: Mouton.

1964b. A Formal Account of the Crow- and Omaha-Type Kinship Terminologies. In W. H. Goodenough, ed., *Explorations in Cultural Anthropology: Essays in Honor of George Peter Murdock*, pp. 351–393. New York: McGraw-Hill.

√ Lowie, R. H.
1929. Relationship Terms. *Encyclopædia Britannica*, 14th ed., vol. 19, pp. 84–86.

Malinowski, Bronislaw

1922. *Argonauts of the Western Pacific*. London: Routledge.

1929. *The Sexual Life of Savages*. London: G. Routledge and Sons.

1930. Parenthood—The Basis of Social Structure. In V. F. Calverston and Samuel D. Schmalhausen, eds., *The New Generation*, pp. 113–168. New York: Macauley.

1935. *Coral Gardens and Their Magic*. 2 vols. London: G. Allen and Unwin.

Marshall, Gloria A.

1968. Marriage: Comparative Analysis. *International Encyclopedia of the Social Sciences*, vol. 10, pp. 8–19. New York: Macmillan and Free Press.

Marshall, Lorna

1959. Marriage among the !Kung Bushmen. *Africa*, vol. 29, pp. 335–364.

Maude, H. E.

1963. *The Evolution of the Gilbertese* Boti: *An Ethnohistorical Interpretation*. Polynesian Society Memoir No. 35.

Maybury-Lewis, David

1960. Parallel Descent and the Apinayé Anomaly. *Southwestern Journal of Anthropology*, vol. 16, pp. 191–216.

Mead, Margaret

1935. *Sex and Temperament in Three Primitive Societies*. New York: William Morrow.

1956. *New Lives for Old: Cultural Transformation—Manus*. New York: William Morrow.

Mencher, Joan

1965. The Nayars of South Malabar. In M. F. Nimkoff, ed., *Comparative Family Systems*, pp. 163–191. Boston: Houghton Mifflin.

Mitchell, William E.

1963. Theoretical Problems in the Concept of the Kindred. *American Anthropologist*, vol. 65, pp. 343–354.

Mogey, John

1963. Introduction: The Family in its Social Setting. In J. Mogey, ed., *Family and Marriage*, pp. 1–6. International Studies in Sociology and Social Anthropology, vol. 1. Leiden: E. J. Brill.

Morgan, Louis H.

1851. *League of the Ho-De-No-Sau-Nee or Iroquois*. (citations from the edition published by Dodd Mead in 1901, reprinted by the Human Relations Area Files, New Haven; 1954.)

1871. *Systems of Consanguinity and Affinity of the Human Family.* Smithsonian Contributions to Knowledge, 17.

1877. *Ancient Society.* Chicago: C. H. Kerr (1878, New York: Holt). (Citations are from the 1963 reprint, New York: World Publishing Company.)

Morris, Charles W.

1938. Foundations of the Theory of Signs. *International Encyclopedia of Unified Science,* vol. 1, no. 2. Chicago: University of Chicago Press.

Muller, Jean-Claude

1969. Preferential Marriage among the Rukuba of Benue-Plateau State, Nigeria. *American Anthropologist,* vol. 71, pp. 1057–1061.

Murdock, George P.

1940. Double Descent. *American Anthropologist,* vol. 42, pp. 555–561.

1945. The Common Denominator of Cultures. In R. Linton, ed., *The Science of Man in the World Crisis,* pp. 123–142. New York: Columbia University Press.

1949. *Social Structure.* New York: Macmillan.

1959. Evolution in Social Organization. In B. J. Meggers, ed., *Evolution and Anthropology,* pp. 126–143. Washington: Anthropological Society of Washington.

1960. Cognatic Forms of Social Organization. In G. P. Murdock, ed., *Social Structure in Southeast Asia.* Viking Fund Publications in Anthropology No. 29. New York: Wenner-Gren Foundation for Anthropological Research.

1967. Ethnographic Atlas: A Summary. *Ethnology,* vol. 6, pp. 109–236.

Murdock, G. P., ed.

1960. *Social Structure in Southeast Asia.* Viking Fund Publications in Anthropology No. 29. New York: Wenner-Gren Foundation for Anthropological Research.

Murdock, G. P., *et al.*

1945. *Outline of Cultural Materials.* Yale Anthropological Studies No. 2.

Murphy, John J.

1954. *The Book of Pidgin English.* 4th ed. Brisbane: W. R. Smith and Paterson.

Nakane, Chie

1963. The Nayar Family in a Disintegrating Matrilineal System. In J. Mogey, ed., *Family and Marriage,* pp. 17–28. International

Studies in Sociology and Social Anthropology, vol. 1. Leiden: E. J. Brill.

Naroll, Raoul

 1964. On Ethnic Unit Classification. *Current Anthropology*, vol. 5, pp. 283–312.

 1967. The Proposed HRAF Probability Sample. *Behavior Science Notes*, vol. 2, pp. 70–80.

Nerlove, Sara, and A. Kimball Romney

 1967. Sibling Terminology and Cross-Sex Behavior. *American Anthropologist*, vol. 69, pp. 179–187.

Netting, Robert McC.

 1969. Women's Weapons: The Politics of Domesticity among the Kofyar. *American Anthropologist*, vol. 71, pp. 1037–1046.

Nimkoff, M. F., ed.

 1965. *Comparative Family Systems*. Boston: Houghton Mifflin.

Nimuendajú, Curt

 1939. *The Apinayé*. Washington: Catholic University of America.

Notes and Queries

 1951. *Notes and Queries in Anthropology*. 6th ed., rev. and rewritten. London: Routledge and Kegan Paul.

Oliver, Douglas

 1955. *A Solomon Island Society*. Cambridge, Mass.: Harvard University Press.

Otterbein, Keith

 1965. Caribbean Family Organization: A Comparative Analysis. *American Anthropologist*, vol. 67, pp. 66–79.

Pehrson, Robert N.

 1957. *The Bilateral Network of Social Relations in Könkämä Lapp District*. Bloomington: Indiana University Research Center in Anthropology, Folklore, and Linguistics.

Peranio, Roger D.

 1961. Descent, Descent Line, and Descent Group in Cognatic Social Systems. *Proceedings of the 1961 Annual Spring Meeting of the American Ethnological Society*, pp. 93–113.

Pike, Kenneth L.

 1943. *Phonetics: A Critical Analysis of Phonetic Theory and a Technic for the Practical Description of Sounds*. Ann Arbor: University of Michigan Press.

 1967. *Language in Relation to a Unified Theory of the Structure of Human Behavior*. 2nd. rev. ed. The Hague: Mouton. (1st ed. 1954, Glendale: Summer Institute of Linguistics.)

Powell, H. A.
n.d. *Trobriand Social Structure*. Unpublished ms.

Radcliffe-Brown, A. R.
1930–31. The Social Organization of Australian Tribes. *Oceania*, vol. 1, pp. 34–63, 206–256, 426–456.
1941. The Study of Kinship Systems. *Journal of the Royal Anthropological Institute*, vol. 71, pp. 1–18.
1950. Introduction. In A. R. Radcliffe-Brown and D. Forde, eds., *African Systems of Kinship and Marriage*, pp. 1–85. London: Oxford University Press.

Rattray, R. S.
1929. *Ashanti Law and Constitution*. Oxford: Clarendon Press.

Reid, Russell M.
1967. Marriage Systems and Algebraic Theory: A Critique of White's *An Anatomy of Kinship*. *American Anthropologist*, vol. 60, pp. 59–74.

Rivers, W. H. R.
1914. *The History of Melanesian Society*. 2 vols. New York: Cambridge University Press.
1924. *Social Organization*. New York: Knopf

Roberts, John M., and Brian Sutton-Smith
1962. Child Training and Game Involvement. *Ethnology*, vol. 1, pp. 166–185.

Romney, A. Kimball
1965. Kalmuk Mongol and the Classification of Lineal Kinship Terminologies. In E. A. Hammel, ed., *Formal Semantic Analysis*, pp. 127–141. Special Publication, *American Anthropologist*, vol. 67, no. 5, part 2.

Romney, A. Kimball, and Philip J. Epling
1958. A Simplified Model of Kariera Kinship. *American Anthropologist*, vol. 60, pp. 59–74.

Sahlins, Marshall D.
1962. *Moala: Culture and Nature on a Fijian Island*. Ann Arbor: The University of Michigan Press.

Sangree, Walter H.
1969. Going Home to Mother: Traditional Marriage Among the Irigwe of Benue-Plateau State, Nigeria. *American Anthropologist*, vol. 71, pp. 1046–1057.

Scheffler, Harold W.
1962. Kindred and Kin Groups in Simbo Island Social Structure. *Ethnology*, vol. 1, pp. 135–157.

1964. Descent Concepts and Descent Groups: The Maori Case. *Journal of the Polynesian Society*, vol. 73, pp. 126–133.

1965. *Choiseul Island Social Structure.* Berkeley and Los Angeles: University of California Press.

√ 1966. Ancestor Worship in Anthropology: or Observations on Descent and Descent Groups. *Current Anthropology*, vol. 7, pp. 541–551.

1970. Kinship and Adoption in the Northern New Hebrides. In V. Carroll, ed., *Adoption in Eastern Oceania,* pp. 369–389. Honolulu: University of California Press.

Schneider, David M.

1953. Yap Kinship Terminology and Kin Groups. *American Anthropologist,* vol. 55, pp. 215–236.

1961. Introduction: The Distinctive Features of Matrilineal Descent Groups. In D. M. Schneider and K. Gough, eds., *Matrilineal Kinship,* pp. 1–29. Berkeley and Los Angeles: University of California Press.

1962. Double Descent on Yap. *Journal of the Polynesian Society,* vol. 71, pp. 1–24.

1964. The Nature of Kinship. *Man,* vol. 64, pp. 180–181.

1965. Some Muddles in the Models: Or, How the System Really Works. In M. Banton, ed., *The Relevance of Models for Social Anthropology,* A.S.A. Monographs 1. New York: Praeger.

1968a. *American Kinship: A Cultural Account.* Englewood Cliffs, N. J.: Prentice-Hall

1968b. Rivers and Kroeber in the Study of Kinship. In W. H. R. Rivers, *Kinship and Social Organization.* London School of Economics Monographs on Social Anthropology No. 34. London: Athlone Press.

1968c. Virgin Birth. *Man,* n.s., vol. 3, pp. 126–129.

Schneider, David M., and Kathleen Gough, eds.

1961. *Matrilineal Kinship.* Berkeley and Los Angeles: University of California Press.

Schwartz, Theodore

1962. *The Paliau Movement in the Admiralty Islands, 1946–1954.* Anthropological Papers of the American Museum of Natural History, vol. 49, part 2.

Service, Elman R.

1962. *Primitive Social Organization: An Evolutionary Perspective.* New York: Random House.

Simmons, Donald C.
   1960. Sexual Life, Marriage, and Childhood among the Efik. *Africa*, vol. 30, pp. 153–165.
Slater, Mirriam Kreiselman
   1959. Ecological Factors in the Origin of Incest. *American Anthropologist*, vol. 61, pp. 1041–1059.
Sledd, James H.
   1962. Lynching the Lexicographers. *Symposium on Language and Culture: Proceedings of the 1962 Annual Spring Meeting of the American Ethnological Society*, pp. 69–95.
Smith, Raymond T.
   1956. *The Negro Family in British Guiana*. London: Routledge and Kegan Paul.
   1962. Culture and Social Structure in the Caribbean: Some Recent Work on Family and Kinship Studies. *Comparative Studies in Society and History*, vol. 6, pp. 24–46.
Solien, Nancie L.
   1959. The Nonunilineal Descent Group in the Caribbean and Central America. *American Anthropologist*, vol. 61, pp. 578–583.
Spier, Leslie
   1925. The Distribution of Kinship Systems in North America. *University of Washington Publications in Anthropology*, no. 1, pp. 69–88.
Spiro, Melford E.
   1954. Is the Family Universal? *American Anthropologist*, vol. 56, pp. 839–846.
Stephens, William N.
   1963. *The Family in Cross-Cultural Perspective*. New York: Holt, Rinehart and Winston.
Sturtevant, William C.
   1964. Studies in Ethnoscience. In A. K. Romney and R. G. D'Andrade, eds., *Transcultural Studies in Cognition*, pp. 99–131. Special Publication, *American Anthropologist*, vol. 66, no. 3, part 2.
Talmon, Yonina
   1965. The Family in a Revolutionary Movement—The Case of the Kibbutz in Israel. In M. F. Nimkoff, ed., *Comparative Family Systems*, pp. 259–286. Boston: Houghton Mifflin.
Textor, Robert B.
   1967. *A Cross-Cultural Summary*. New Haven: HRAF Press.

Tylor, E. B.
  1889. On a Method of Investigating the Development of Institutions. *Journal of the Royal Anthropological Institute,* vol. 18, pp. 245–272.

Whiting, John W. M., and Irving L. Child
  1953. *Child Training and Personality: A Cross-Cultural Study.* New Haven: Yale University Press.

Williamson, Kay
  1962. Changes in the Marriage System of the Okrika Ijo. *Africa,* vol. 32, pp. 53–60.

Winch, Robert F.
  1968. Marriage: Family Formation. *International Encyclopedia of the Social Sciences* vol. 10, pp. 1–8. New York: Macmillan and Free Press.

Wissler, Clark
  1917. *The American Indian.* New York: McMurtrie.
  1923. *Man and Culture.* New York: Thomas Y. Crowell.
  1926. *The Relation of Nature to Man in Aboriginal America.* New York: Oxford.

Wolf, Arthur P.
  1966. Childhood Association, Sexual Attraction, and the Incest Taboo: A Chinese Case. *American Anthropologist,* vol. 68, pp. 883–898.

Yalman, Nur
  1962. The Structure of the Sinhalese Kindred: A Re-Examination of the Dravidian Terminology. *American Anthropologist,* vol. 64, pp. 548–575.
  1967. *Under the Bo Tree: Studies in Caste, Kinship, and Kinship and Marriage in the Interior of Ceylon.* Berkeley: University of California Press.

Young, Michael W.
  1968. Bwaidogan Descent Groups. *American Anthropologist,* vol. 60, pp. 333–336.

Index